Code 23

MW01707869

The Business Strategy Game

A Global Industry Simulation

6th Edition

Player's Manual

Created by
Arthur A. Thompson, Jr.
Gregory J. Stappenbeck
The University of Alabama

Irwin McGraw-Hill

Boston Burr Ridge, IL Dubuque, IA Madison, WI
New York San Francisco St. Louis
Bangkok Bogotá Caracas Lisbon London Madrid Mexico City
Milan New Delhi Seoul Singapore Sydney Taipei Toronto

Irwin/McGraw-Hill

A Division of The ***McGraw-Hill*** *Companies*

Player's Manual to accompany
THE BUSINESS STRATEGY GAME: A GLOBAL INDUSTRY SIMULATION
International Editions 2000

10 9 8 7 6 5 4 3 2 1
20 9 8 7 6 5 4 3 2 1 0 9
SLP UPE

Package ISBN 0-07-116909-1
Manual ISBN 0-07-116869-9
Disk pack ISBN 0-07-116870-2

www.mhhe.com

Printed in Singapore

TABLE OF CONTENTS

SECTION 1: THE INDUSTRY AND THE COMPANY **1**
What You Can Expect to Learn 2
The Company and Its Product Line 3
Company Background 4
The Industry and Competitive Environment 7
Industry Sales Projections for Years 11 and 12 7
Customers and Distribution Channels 9
Raw Material Supplies 10
Manufacturing 11
Weapons of Competitive Rivalry 11
Competitive Strategy Options 16

SECTION 2: COMPANY OPERATIONS AND REPORTS **17**
The Manufacturing Report 18
The Warehouse and Sales Report 25
The Marketing and Administrative Report 30
The Geographic Profit Report 31
The Cost Report 32
The Income Statement 35
The Balance Sheet 36
The Cash Flow Report 38
Using the Company Reports 39

SECTION 3: STRATEGIES AND DECISIONS **41**
Pertinent Strategic Issues 41
Pertinent Operating Issues 42
Prevailing Costs and Rates 43
Making Decisions 44
Manufacturing Decisions 44
Labor Decisions 49
Shipping Decisions 51
Plant Decisions 53
Private-Label Marketing Decisions 57
Branded Marketing Decisions 59
The Demand Forecasting Model 61
The Inventory Liquidation Option 63
Bids for New Celebrity Endorsement Contracts 64
Financial Decisions 65
Executive Compensation Decision (optional screen) 70
The Decision Menu Bar 72
The Projections at the Bottom of Each Screen 73
Reaching a “Final” Set of Decisions 73

TABLE OF CONTENTS (continued)

SECTION 4: SCORING, REPORTS, AND STRATEGIC PLANS 75
Scoring Your Company's Performance 75
The Footwear Industry Report 78
The Benchmarking Report 79
Competitor Analysis Reports 79
Company Reports Containing This Year's Results 80
Looking Ahead: The Five-Year Strategic Plan Menu Option 80

SECTION 5: USING THE COMPANY PROGRAMS AND DISKS 81
Hardware Requirements 81
Installing the Company Program Disk on Your PC 82
Operating Your Company 82
Identifying Your Company 83
Exploring the Main Menu 84
Recommended Decision-Making Procedures 86
Concluding Comments 88

APPENDIX A: SAMPLE INDUSTRY REPORTS 89
Sample Footwear Industry Report 90
Sample Benchmarking Report 101
Sample Competitor Analysis Reports 102

APPENDIX B: PLANNING AND ANALYSIS FORMS 105
Company Mission and Objectives Form 107
Company Strategy Form 109
Industry and Competitive Analysis Form 111

INDEX 115

Section 1

THE INDUSTRY AND THE COMPANY

Welcome to *The Business Strategy Game*! You are joining the senior management team at an $83 million company making athletic footwear. Not only is the company's product line gaining in popularity with consumers, but the athletic footwear industry is also on the verge of rapid growth worldwide. You and your co-managers have the challenge of developing and executing a strategy that will propel the company into a leading position in the North American, European, and Asian markets over the next 5 to 10 years. Your company will be in head-on competition with a number of other companies seeking to capture this same market potential.

In playing *The Business Strategy Game*, you and your co-managers will need to address a number of strategic and operating issues. Immediate problems include making the company's recent entry into the Asian market a profitable success, dealing with high production costs at the company's Ohio plant, and meeting growing demand for the company's footwear products in the world's three major geographic markets — North America, Europe, and Asia. Longer range, the challenge will be to build a sustainable competitive advantage and maneuver the company into an industry-leading position. As competition in the marketplace unfolds, you will be pressed to devise actions to defend your company's market position against the competitive offensives of rival firms, and you will have to consider what counteroffensives to launch on your own.

You and your co-managers will have full authority over the company's selling prices, product quality, customer service effort, advertising, product line breadth, retail outlet network, and promotional rebate offers, thus giving you an array of competitive strategy options in each market segment in which you decide to compete. It will be entirely up to you and your co-managers to decide how to try to outcompete rival companies — whether to strive to become the industry's low-cost producer and use your low-cost advantage to undersell competitors, whether to differentiate your company's footwear lineup on the basis of quality or service or other attributes, and whether to compete worldwide or to focus on just one or two market segments. You can elect to position the company in the low end of the market, the high end, or stick close to the middle on price, quality, and service. You can put the marketing emphasis on brand-name footwear or you can stress sales to private-label retailers. You can stick to a North American production base or you can build new plants in Europe and/or Asia. And, you can finance the company's growth with whatever mix of cash, short-term loans, long-term bonds, or new issues of common stock that you deem appropriate. Whichever long-term direction and business strategy is chosen, you and your co-managers will be held accountable for achieving acceptable financial performance, increasing shareholder value, and making the company a recognized industry leader. The success your executive team has in managing the company will be based on how well your company compares against other companies on six performance measures: sales revenues, after-tax profits, return on equity, bond rating, stock value, and strategy rating.

Each decision period in *The Business Strategy Game* represents a year. Very likely, you and your co-managers will be asked to make anywhere from 6 to 12 complete sets of decisions, meaning that you will be in charge of the company for 6-12 years — long enough to test your strategy-making, strategy-implementing skills. Expect the action to be fast-paced and exciting as industry conditions change and as companies jockey for market position and competitive advantage.

What You Can Expect to Learn

The Business Strategy Game is a hands-on learning exercise that will give you valuable decision-making practice and develop your powers of business judgment. In making the strategic and operating decisions that arise in the simulation, you and your co-managers will encounter an array of fairly typical business issues. You'll encounter a need to assess changing industry and competitive conditions, diagnose the strategies of competitors and anticipate their next moves, pursue ways to secure a competitive advantage, evaluate different courses of action, chart a strategic course for your company to take, and adjust strategic plans in response to changing conditions. There will be ample opportunities to gain proficiency in using the concepts and tools of strategic analysis. You will learn what it means to "think strategically" about a company's competitive market position and the kinds of actions it will take to improve it. As your skills in "market-watching" and "competitor-watching" get sharper, your sense of business judgment about how to strengthen a company's competitive position and financial performance will improve. You will get to test your ideas about how to run a company, and there will be prompt feedback on the caliber of your decisions.

Second, you will gain a stronger understanding of how the different functional pieces of a business (production, marketing, finance, and so on) fit together, thus integrating the knowledge from other business courses you have taken. *The Business Strategy Game* draws upon many of the standard topics you have studied in your production, marketing, finance, accounting, human resources, and economics courses. The company you will be managing has plants to operate, work forces to hire and pay, inventories to control, marketing and sales campaigns to wage, prices to set, accounting and cost data to examine, capital expenditure and investment decisions to make, shareholders to worry about, sales forecasts to decide upon, tariffs and exchange rate fluctuations to consider, and ups and downs in interest rates and the stock and bond markets to take into account. So there is a bit of everything in *The Business Strategy Game* — it is a "big picture" experience that requires looking at decisions from a ***total-company perspective*** and unifying decisions in a variety of functional areas to create a cohesive strategic action plan. You'll learn why and how decisions made in one area affect outcomes in other areas of the company. All the while, you and your co-managers will be held accountable for keeping the company profitable, earning an adequate return on equity investment, protecting the company's bond rating, endeavoring to maximize shareholder wealth via increased dividend payments and stock price appreciation, and developing an effective business strategy. You will have to live with your decisions — for better or for worse.

Third, *The Business Strategy Game* will give you more insight into the ins and outs of global competition, the different strategies companies can pursue in world markets, and the challenges of competing in a global market environment. We have designed *The Business Strategy Game* to be as realistic and as faithful to the functioning of a worldwide competitive market as a computerized simulation exercise can be. The game brings into play many of the business issues and competitive conditions characteristic of today's global markets. Your company will have to contend with exchange rate fluctuations, tariff barriers, and production cost differences. You will have to decide whether to locate plants where wage rates are low or whether to avoid import tariffs by having a production base in each primary geographic market. You will learn what it means to compete against low-cost, foreign-made goods.

Fourth, playing *The Business Strategy Game* will boost your understanding of basic revenue-cost-profit relationships. The what-iffing and numerical analysis that you'll find essential in operating your company in a businesslike manner will give you far greater command of the numbers commonly found in business reports. You'll get valuable practice in reviewing operating statistics, identifying costs that are out-of-line, comparing the profitability of different market segments, assessing your company's financial condition, and deciding on what remedial and proactive approaches to take. Since the simulation is played on personal computers, the nitty-gritty number-crunching is done in a split second with only a few keystrokes. This makes it simple and quick to do all kinds of "what-iffing" and explore which of several decision options seems to offer the most profit potential. You will be able to construct one-year and five-year strategic plans with relative ease, obtain immediate estimates of the financial performance you can expect, and evaluate the tradeoffs between short-run and long-run performance. You'll grow to appreciate the importance of basing decisions on solid number-crunching analysis instead of the quicksand of "I think. . .", "I believe. . .", and "Maybe, it will work out O.K."

In sum, playing *The Business Strategy Game* will build your confidence in analyzing the revenue-cost-profit economics of a business, help you understand how the functional pieces of a business fit together, and develop your powers of managerial judgment. You will gain needed experience and practice in assessing business risk, analyzing industry and competitive conditions, making decisions from a companywide perspective, thinking strategically about a company's situation and future prospects, developing strategies and revising them in light of changing conditions, and applying what you have learned in business school. The bottom line is that playing *The Business Strategy Game* will make you better prepared for playing the game of business in real life. We predict that in the process your competitive spirit will be stimulated and that you will have a lot of fun.

THE COMPANY AND ITS PRODUCT LINE

You and your co-managers have been chosen by the Board of Directors to take charge of the company's rapidly expanding athletic footwear business. Over the past few years, the company has strengthened its market position; it is well situated to capitalize on growth opportunities in North America, Europe, and Asia (Australia, New Zealand, China, Japan, South Korea, and other Pacific Rim countries). The Board of Directors expects you to manage the company in a manner that will:

- make the company a leader in the athletic footwear industry and
- build shareholder value via both higher dividends and a rising stock price.

The Board has given you wide-ranging authority to institute whatever strategic actions and operating changes you decide are appropriate.

COMPANY BACKGROUND

The company was founded 10 years ago in Ohio by John Delgaudio, Richard Tebo, and Walter Ruggles to manufacture and market running and jogging shoes. John and Richard had tried various brands of track shoes while members of the track team at a well-known mid-western university. Both had experienced shoe-related difficulties of one sort or another and felt that no company made shoes that provided good foot protection and that performed well under the conditions encountered in cross country running and in long-distance marathons run on hard pavement. Long discussions about what they were going to do after graduation led them to think about forming a small company of their own to develop and market a new-style shoe line with features that would be welcomed by runners and serious joggers.

John's father had been a manufacturer's representative for one of the traditional athletic equipment companies ever since John was in the second grade. When John and Richard began to talk in earnest about starting their own athletic shoe company, John's father arranged for John and Richard to spend a day touring one of the New England shoe plants operated by the manufacturer he represented. It was during this trip that John and Richard met Walter Ruggles, who at age 32 had risen quickly through the ranks to become plant manager. Walter had a degree in mechanical engineering and was fascinated with machinery and the technical manufacturing aspects of the footwear-making process. The three young men hit it off well together, and John and Richard immediately decided to invite Walter to join them in exploring the possibility of setting up their own company.

Two months after John and Richard graduated, plans for the new company were in high gear. Hours of brainstorming and intensive study of shoes then on the market produced three shoe designs with features no other manufacturer had. One feature involved a special air cushion sole, another involved the use of a waterproof fabric that breathed and wicked away foot perspiration, and a third involved a new type of heel support. Walter's technical know-how proved invaluable in drawing up designs and figuring out how to manufacture the shoes. Meanwhile, John located some used manufacturing equipment in reasonably good condition that could be leased for $5,000 per month with an option to buy.

Attention then centered on two things: a site for a small plant and raising the $35,000 which the partners needed to get started on a small scale. Richard came from a well-to-do family that owned a number of business enterprises in southern Ohio. One of the Tebo companies happened to have a 15,000 square-foot warehouse on the edge of the downtown Cincinnati area that was temporarily vacant. Richard's parents agreed to rent-free use of the warehouse for a six-month period. The matter of the $35,000 was surmounted in the form of $20,000 in savings which Walter had accumulated and $15,000 which John borrowed from his father. Tebo's parents agreed to lend the company up to $50,000 for working capital until the company's financial statements were strong enough to negotiate bank loans on its own.

THE FIRST FIVE YEARS. The company was formally incorporated in August, with each founder having a one-third ownership. The group agreed that John Delgaudio would function in the role of president and handle the financial and administrative chores; Richard Tebo took charge of the distribution and sales functions; and Walter Ruggles assumed responsibility for product design, purchasing, and manufacturing operations. The first pair of shoes rolled off the production line in mid-October and the first shipment to a retail dealer was personally delivered by Richard Tebo the week before Thanksgiving, just in time for the Christmas shopping season.

The first two years were a struggle — long hours were spent testing various features and types of materials, perfecting shoe designs for different activities (jogging, walking, tennis, and track), working the bugs out of the makeshift equipment and plant setup, demonstrating the shoes to dealers, and convincing dealers to handle the company's shoe line. Hundreds of pairs were given away free to high school athletes to try; Tebo spent many hours listening to user reactions and monitoring how well the shoes held up under wear and tear. The company lost money in its first year and had to use nearly $32,000 of the $50,000 loan extended by Richard Tebo's parents. But the shoes coming off the assembly line were looking better, manufacturing efficiency was improving, and reaction to the company's shoes was positive. In the second year of operation, the company sold a total of 28,000 pairs and revenues topped $500,000. Most of the sales were to independent retail dealers in the southern Ohio and northern Kentucky areas. Richard Tebo's persistence in calling on these dealers frequently, explaining the features of the shoe models to them, and even assisting the store clerks in selling customers on the shoes were a big factor in giving the company a market toehold.

In the company's third year of operation, cash flows improved and the company's financial status grew less precarious. Pairs sold topped 150,000 and revenues surpassed the $3 million mark. The founders plowed all their profits back into the business, concentrating on designing more models, obtaining additional manufacturing equipment, and broadening geographic distribution. The Cincinnati warehouse housing the company's operations was purchased from the Tebo family. The company concentrated on selling its line of athletic footwear to sporting goods stores. Then as teenagers and young adults began the trend to wear tennis shoes and jogging shoes instead of leather shoes for everyday, walking-around purposes, the company started marketing to retail shoe stores as well as athletic stores. A line of walking shoes for men and women was introduced.

By the company's fourth year of operation, market demand for athletic footwear started to take off in the United States and Europe. The rising price of leather shoes made fabric shoes an attractive money-saving option. At the same time, dress styles were becoming more casual among adults, and more people of all ages were taking up jogging, walking, aerobics, and regular exercise. Athletic footwear became a standard item in people's personal wardrobes. Meanwhile, the Ohio plant was expanded to a capacity of 1,000,000 pairs annually and a comfortable casual-wear line of shoes for men, women, and children was introduced. In Year 5, demand for the company's brand jumped to 775,000 pairs and revenues rose to $17 million.

THE SECOND FIVE YEARS. Over the last five years footwear sales have expanded threefold to almost 2.5 million pairs; revenues for Year 10 totaled $82.8 million. To achieve this growth, the company took some aggressive steps. In Year 6, the co-founders decided to construct an ultra-modern 1,000,000-pair plant with state-of-the-art manufacturing equipment. The new plant, which cost $20 million, was located on the outskirts of San Antonio, Texas, to take advantage of ample supplies of low-cost labor in the area. At the end of Year 8 the Texas plant was expanded to a capacity of 2,000,000 pairs annually. A central distribution center was leased in Memphis, Tennessee, to handle all shipments to retail dealers in North America.

The company leased a warehouse in Brussels, Belgium, to handle distribution of the company's brands throughout the European Community; sales to European dealers began in Year 7 when the Texas plant came on line. Also in Year 7 the company began to supply private-label athletic footwear to such chains as Sears, J. C. Penney, Wal-Mart, and K mart on a competitive bid basis; the company uses the Memphis warehouse to handle all shipments of private label shoes. Most recently, the company has opened a distribution center in Singapore to handle sales to dealers in Japan, South Korea, China, Taiwan, Hong Kong, Indochina, Malaysia, Australia, New Zealand, and other countries in Southeast Asia; sales to dealers in the Asian Pacific began on a small scale this past year. So far, all shipments to Europe and Asia have been made from the company's Texas plant.

To finance the company's rapid expansion program, the company went public in Year 7; 2,000,000 shares were sold to outside investors at a net of $5.00 each. The co-founders own a combined 3,000,000 shares, giving the company a total of 5,000,000 shares of stock outstanding. The stock sale proceeds, along with an $18 million bond issue in Year 7 and another $15 million bond issue in Year 9 were used to finance construction and expansion of the Texas plant and provide working capital.

Table 1-1 summarizes the company's performance for Years 6 through 10 — ***all figures are in thousands*** except for earnings per share and dividends per share. As you can see, the company's growth has been profitable. Earnings per share have risen at a brisk clip, from $0.41 in Year 7 to $1.50 in Year 10. Return on equity investment (ROE) has climbed steadily since Year 6 to 20.0 percent. The company is in good financial shape and has a strong BBB bond rating.

TABLE 1-1: COMPANY PERFORMANCE SUMMARY, YEARS 6 – 10

		Year 6	Year 7	Year 8	Year 9	Year 10
Income Statement Summary:						
Sales Revenues —	Branded	$21,675	$31,958	$41,662	$55,194	$68,640
	Private-Label	0	4,990	9,012	9,485	14,170
	Total	21,675	36,948	50,675	64,679	82,810
Operating Costs –	Manufacturing	15,340	25,987	34,094	43,706	50,433
	Warehouse	2,030	4,034	5,079	6,318	10,407
	Marketing	919	2,063	2,913	3,624	6,081
	Administrative	1,453	1,556	2,169	2,328	2,500
	Total	19,741	33,641	44,256	55,976	69,420
Operating Profit (Loss)		1,934	3,307	6,419	8,703	13,390
Extraordinary Gain (Loss)		0	0	0	0	0
Interest Income (Expense)		0	(347)	(1,774)	(1,584)	(2,702)
Income (Loss) Before Taxes		1,934	2,960	4,645	7,119	10,687
Income Taxes		580	888	1,394	2,136	3,206
Net Income (Loss)		$1,354	$2,072	$3,252	$4,983	$7481
Financial Performance Summary:						
Ending Cash Balance		$493	$1,954	$2874	$1,397	$311
Total Assets		$21,264	$44,785	$4690	$65,208	$69,242
Short-Term Debt		3,500	0	0	0	500
Long-Term Debt		0	18,000	16,200	29,400	26,100
Total Liabilities		4,910	20,359	19,283	33,297	31,850
Total Stockholders' Equity		$16,354	$24,426	$27,677	$31,911	$37,392
Shares of Stock Outstanding		3,000	5,000	5,000	5,000	5,000
Earnings Per Share		$0.45	$0.41	$0.65	$1.00	$1.50
Dividends Per Share		$0.00	$0.00	$0.00	$0.15	$0.40
Return On Equity		8.3%	8.5%	11.7%	15.6%	20.0%
Operating Profit Margin		8.9%	8.9%	12.7%	13.5%	16.2%
After-Tax Profit Margin		6.2%	5.6%	6.4%	7.7%	9.0%
Debt-To-Asset Ratio		0.16	0.40	0.34	0.45	0.38
Times-Interest-Earned			9.54	3.62	5.49	4.96
Bond Rating			A	BBB	BB	BBB

The three co-founders — John Delgaudio, Richard Tebo, and Walter Ruggles — have now decided to withdraw from active management of the company. They will remain on the Board of Directors and help set broad policy guidelines, but they are relinquishing decision-making control to you and your co-managers. While they have done a very creditable job of creating an innovative line of running, jogging, walking, and casual wear shoes (a total of 100 models/styles), getting the Texas plant operational, and launching international sales, they are uncertain what sort of long-term strategy the company should follow to become a major player in the world footwear industry. They have discussed at length whether the company can continue to be successful in international markets with a U.S.-only production base. They are unsure whether to expand the company's 100-model product line to include shoes for other types of activities such as basketball, tennis, golf, softball, soccer, and aerobics.

At present, the company doesn't have a well-defined strategy for competing in the world's three major geographic markets; the founders were unable to reach a consensus on whether to follow the same strategy worldwide or whether to pursue separate strategies in North America, Europe, and Asia. Moreover, they didn't agree on whether to position the company as a top-quality, premium-priced producer or as a low-cost producer competing mainly at the low-priced end of the market or as a medium priced seller of an average quality shoe. They were unsure whether it made good economic sense to construct plants in Europe or Asia. They have wavered back and forth on the issues of whether to expand the product line and to contract with sports celebrities to endorse the company's brand. Their indecision on these and other key strategic issues has prompted them to bring you and your co-managers in to run the company and decide what strategic course to pursue.

The Industry and Competitive Environment

The prospects for long-term industrywide growth in footwear sales are excellent. Athletic shoes have become the footwear of choice for children and teenagers, except for dressy occasions. Increased adult concerns regarding physical fitness are boosting adult purchases for use in exercise and recreational activities. At the same time, greater numbers of adults are purchasing athletic footwear for leisure and casual use, attracted by the lower prices in comparison to leather shoes, the greater comfort, and the easy-care features. The comfort aspects have proved very attractive to people who spend a lot of time on their feet and to older people with foot problems. The combined effect of these factors is projected to generate strong market growth in all three major geographic markets over the next five years (Years 11 - 15):

Projected Annual Growth in Pairs Demanded

North America	Europe	Asia
5 – 20%	10 – 25%	15 – 25%

The lower projected growth for the North American market is due to the fact that a sizable fraction of North American consumers have already purchased one or more pairs of athletic shoes, thus making sales more a function of replacement demand than first-time purchases. A more definite five-year demand forecast for the industry is being prepared and will be published in the Footwear Industry Report, a copy of which you will receive at the end of each year (beginning in Year 11).

Industry Sales Projections for Years 11 and 12

Worldwide footwear demand is reliably forecasted to grow 20% in Year 11 and 25% in Year 12, with per company demand averaging 3,000,000 pairs in Year 11 and 3,750,000 pairs in Year 12. The forecasts for the four market segments are:

	Private-Label Demand (in pairs)	Branded Demand (in pairs) North America	Europe	Asia	Worldwide Demand (in pairs)
Year 11	600,000	1,450,000	600,000	350,000	3,000,000
Year 12	700,000	1,820,000	780,000	450,000	3,750,000

It is quite unlikely, however, that your company's actual sales in Years 11 and 12 will turn out to be exactly equal to the above company averages. ***How many pairs your company will actually sell in a given year always depends on how your company's overall competitive effort stacks up against the competitive efforts of rival companies.*** Any company can sell substantially ***more*** than the per-company average by out-competing rival companies. Companies with attractively priced, aggressively marketed products will outsell companies having comparatively over-priced, under-marketed products.

To determine the overall size of the market your company will be competing for in Years 11 and 12, multiply the forecasted quantities per company by the number of companies in your industry.

While the industry sales forecasts for Years 11 and 12 (and the updated five-year forecasts you will receive in each issue of The Footwear Industry Report) should be considered very reliable information, actual industrywide sales in any market segment can deviate from forecasted levels for either of two reasons: (1) unforeseen changes in economic conditions and consumer spending levels and (2) unusually strong or weak competitive efforts on the part of rival companies to capture the available sales volume.

THE ROLE OF THE S&P 500 INDEX. Past experience shows that sales of athletic footwear vary up or down from the market forecast according to changes in the worldwide level of economic activity, consumer confidence, and employment levels. An important new study shows that the sizes of the deviations from forecasted demand correlate very closely with changes in the S&P 500 Index — a much-watched measure of the prices of the common stocks of 500 companies selected by Standard & Poor's.[1] When the S&P 500 has risen above the prior year's value, actual footwear demand industrywide ***in the following year*** has consistently been *above* the forecasted amount. When the S&P 500 has dropped, next year's footwear demand has consistently been *below* the projected volume. The bigger the up or down move in the S&P 500, the bigger the deviations from forecast have been, although the next year's forecast has never been off by more than 10%.

During the upcoming years you should expect ups and downs in the S&P 500 Index to signal that actual industry sales of footwear will deviate above or below the forecast. Just how big a change in the S&P 500 it takes to induce each 1% deviation from the forecasted footwear volume is still unclear, but astute company managers should be able to arrive at good estimates within a short time. The size of the deviation from the forecasted amount depends on how much the S&P 500 Index moves above or below the value announced by the instructor/game administrator for the previous year. If the upcoming year's S&P 500 value exceeds the prior-year value, actual market demand will be larger than forecasted market demand. The bigger the gap between the current year's S&P 500 and the previous year's S&P 500 value, the larger that the actual number of pairs demanded will exceed the forecasted volume (subject to the 10% limit). Conversely, actual market demand will fall below the forecasted demand when the current year's S&P 500 value falls below the previous year's value.

The maximum effect that changes in the S&P 500 can have on next year's worldwide footwear demand is ±10%.

[1] *The daily changes in the S & P 500 Index can be found on the first page of the third section of The Wall Street Journal; it is also reported in the business section of many newspapers.*

THE ROLE OF COMPETITIVE AGGRESSIVENESS. Actual industry sales of athletic shoes are also a function of how aggressively all companies as a group try to capture the projected sales volumes. A ***significant*** drop in footwear prices can stimulate buying and cause actual sales to rise above the forecasted amounts. Likewise, if companies as a group ***significantly*** boost product quality or improve customer service, then sales for the year can exceed the projected amounts. ***Unusually aggressive price-cutting and marketing industrywide can boost actual market volume by as much as 4% over the projected amount.***

> ***Unusually aggressive (unaggressive) pricing and marketing industrywide will increase (decrease) actual sales volumes above (below) projected amounts.***

On the other hand, ***if average prices for footwear rise sharply or footwear quality drops or marketing efforts are cut to minimal levels, then buyers may not be attracted to purchase as many pairs as forecasted.*** The weaker the industry's overall competitive effort, the greater the amount by which actual sales can fall below forecasted volumes. ***All sales volume projections are based on the assumption that companies will present products comparable to the price-quality-model mix offered in Year 10, and that companies will exert promotional efforts comparable to Year 10 levels.***

CUSTOMERS AND DISTRIBUTION CHANNELS

The ultimate customers for athletic footwear, of course, are the people who wear the shoes. But athletic footwear manufacturers have all refrained from integrating forward into retailing and making direct sales to the final user. The preferred channel for accessing consumers is through retailers who carry athletic footwear — department stores, retail shoe stores, sporting goods stores, and pro shops at golf and tennis clubs. Each manufacturer in the industry has created a brand name for its shoe line and built a network of retailers to handle its brand in all three geographic markets. Retailers are recruited and serviced by independent sales representatives (sometimes called manufacturer's representatives) who are paid on a straight 10% commission basis. Each company has sales reps to handle its product line exclusively in each geographic market. The role of sales reps is to call on retailers, convince them of the merits to carrying the company's brand of footwear, assist them with merchandising and in-store displays, and solicit orders. Manufacturers gain consumer awareness of their brands via in-store displays of retailers, media advertising, and word-of-mouth.

In the North American market only, there's a second distribution channel — private-label sales to large chain store accounts. Certain chains prefer to sell athletic footwear under their own label at prices 20% to 30% below manufacturers' name brands. These chains buy their private-label merchandise from manufacturers on a competitive-bid basis in lots of 50,000 pairs. All chain stores specify minimum quality and product variety; the bids of manufacturers who cannot meet quality and style specifications are automatically rejected even if their bid prices are lower. During the past three years chain stores have purchased private-label shoes at prices of $2.50 to $5.35 per pair lower than the average wholesale prices manufacturers have charged retail dealers for name brand footwear. ***The maximum price that chain store buyers will pay for private-label footwear is $2.50 under the average North American wholesale price manufacturers charge for branded footwear — without a price break of at least $2.50 per pair, they believe they're better off selling name brands.***

The typical footwear retailer sells name brand shoes at a price that is double the wholesale price of manufacturers, whereas private-label footwear retails for a markup of only 70% over the price paid to manufacturers. The lower wholesale price which your company and other footwear manufacturers charge for private-label footwear reflects (1) lower costs — manufacturers incur essentially no marketing costs on private-label footwear sales and (2) competition for the business of chain retailers.

Customer demand for athletic footwear is diverse in terms of price, quality, and types of models. There are customers who are satisfied with no frills budget-priced shoes and there are customers who are quite willing to pay premium prices for top-of-the-line quality, multiple features, and fashionable styling. The biggest market segment consists of customers who use their shoes for general wear, but there are sizable buyer segments for specialty shoes designed expressly for tennis, golf, jogging, aerobics, basketball, soccer, bowling, and so on. The diversity of buyer demand gives manufacturers room to pursue a variety of strategies — from competing across-the-board with many models and below-average prices to making a limited number of styles for buyers willing to pay premium prices for top-of-the-line quality.

RAW MATERIAL SUPPLIES

All of the materials used in producing athletic footwear are readily available on the open market. There are some 300 different suppliers worldwide who have the capability to furnish interior lining fabrics, waterproof fabrics and plastics for external use, rubber and plastic materials for soles, shoelaces, and high-strength thread. It is substantially cheaper for footwear manufacturers to purchase these materials from outside suppliers than it is to manufacture them internally in the small volumes needed. Delivery time on all materials is a matter of one or two days, allowing manufacturers to stock less than five days' worth of inventories.

Suppliers offer two basic grades of raw materials: normal-wear and long-wear. The use of long-wear fabrics and shoe sole materials improves shoe quality and performance, but they currently cost about twice as much as normal-wear components. Materials for a shoe made completely of long-wear components cost $12 per pair versus a cost of $6 per pair for shoes made entirely of normal-wear components. However, ***shoes can be manufactured with any percentage combination of normal-wear and long-wear materials.*** All footwear-making equipment in present and future plants will accommodate a mixture of normal-wear and long-wear components.

All materials suppliers charge the going market price, and the quality of long-wear and normal-wear materials is the same from supplier to supplier. Materials prices fluctuate according to worldwide supply-demand conditions. ***Whenever worldwide shoe production falls below 90% of the footwear industry's worldwide plant capacity (not counting overtime production capability), the market prices for both normal and long-wear materials drop 1% for each 1% below the 90% capacity utilization level.*** Such price reductions reflect weak demand and increased competition among materials suppliers for the available orders. Conversely, ***whenever worldwide shoe production exceeds 100% of worldwide plant capacity utilization (meaning that companies, on average, are producing at overtime), the market prices for normal and long-wear materials rise 1% for each 1% that worldwide capacity utilization exceeds 100%.*** Such price increases reflect strong demand for materials and greater ability on the part of suppliers to get away with charging more for essential raw materials.

> ***Materials prices fluctuate according to worldwide utilization of plant capacity and the percentage use of long-wear materials.***

A second demand-supply condition causing materials prices to change is widespread substitution of long-wear materials for normal-wear materials. ***Once industrywide usage of long-wear materials passes the 25% level, the prices of long-wear materials rise 0.5% for each 1% that the percentage use of long-wear materials exceeds 25%; simultaneously, the worldwide market price of normal-wear materials will fall 0.5% for each 1% that the industrywide usage of normal-wear materials falls below 75%.*** Thus the price gap between long-wear and normal-wear materials widens as industrywide use of long-wear materials rises above 25%.

Despite price fluctuations, materials suppliers have ample capacity to furnish whatever volume of materials footwear manufacturers need. No shortages have occurred in the past. Just recently, suppliers indicated they would have no difficulty in accommodating increased materials demand in the event footwear-makers build additional plant capacity to meet the growing demand for athletic-style shoes. ***Footwear manufacturers are thus assured of receiving all orders for normal-wear and long-wear materials*** no matter how much new footwear capacity is built down the road.

MANUFACTURING

Footwear manufacturing has evolved into a rather uncomplicated process, and the technology has matured to the point where it is well understood throughout the industry. At present, no company has proprietary know-how that translates into manufacturing advantage. The production process consists of cutting fabrics and materials to conform to size and design patterns, stitching the various pieces of the shoe top together, molding and gluing the shoe soles, binding the shoe top to the sole, and inserting the innersole and laces. Tasks are divided among production workers in such a manner that it is easy to measure individual worker output and thus create incentive compensation tied to piecework. Labor productivity is determined more by worker dexterity and effort than by machine speed; this is why ***piecework incentives can induce greater output per worker***. On the other hand, there is ample room for worker error; unless workers pay careful attention to detail, the quality of workmanship in the final product suffers. ***Quality control procedures at each step of the process are essential to minimizing the reject rates on pairs produced.***

Studies have shown that assembly lines are most efficient producing only one model at a time, though it is easy to produce different sizes of the same model simultaneously. To switch production over from one model to another takes several hours of set-up time and usually is done between shifts. Machine maintenance is also done between regular work shifts. There is sufficient time after allowing for maintenance and production setup for new models to accommodate overtime production up to 20% of normal production capacity. Thus a plant capable of producing 1 million pairs annually with a normal 40-hour work week can turn out 1.2 million pairs annually with the maximum 20% use of overtime.

> ***A plant may operate under overtime conditions up to a maximum of 20% above its normal annual production capacity.***

Industry observers are predicting that companies will take a hard look at the economics of producing athletic shoes in Asian countries where trainable supplies of low-wage labor are readily available. Wages and benefits for Asian workers start at $2,500 annually compared to $9,000 in Europe and $10,000 or more in North America. The basic shoe-making abilities of workers in Asia, Europe, and North America are roughly equal since only modest labor skills are needed and training periods for workers are short. However, worker productivity levels at different plants can vary substantially due to the use of different incentive compensation plans, different production methods, and different automation options.

WEAPONS OF COMPETITIVE RIVALRY

Competition among footwear producers centers around eight sales-determining variables: wholesale selling price, product quality, service, product line breadth, the number of retail outlets handling each company's brand, advertising, celebrity endorsements and brand image, and use of customer rebates. Each company's market share in a given geographic area (North America, Europe, Asia) depends on how its combined use of the eight competitive weapons stacks up against the competitive effort of other companies competing in the same region. The stronger a company's overall competitive effort is relative to rival companies, the more pairs the company will sell and the larger its market share in that geographic region will be (provided, of course, that it has produced enough pairs to meet demand). It is essential that you understand the role and impact of each of the eight weapons of competitive rivalry.

WHOLESALE SELLING PRICE. This is the most important of the eight competitive factors. The higher your company's wholesale price to retailers, the higher the prices that retailers will charge consumers. Consumers are quite knowledgeable about the prices of different brands, and many do comparison shopping on price before settling upon a brand to purchase. If your company's wholesale price in a geographic area is above the industry average in that area, some shoppers who otherwise are attracted to your brand will switch to lower-priced brands. The more your company's wholesale selling price is above the geographic average, the bigger the percentage of sales your company stands to lose to competitors. However, a higher-than-average selling price can be partially or wholly offset by a combination of higher product quality, better service to retailers, extra advertising, bigger customer rebates, the use of celebrity endorsements, the addition of more models to your company's product line, and a larger network of retail outlets. But the higher your company's prices are above the industry average, the harder it is to overcome buyer resistance and avoid a loss in market share.

> ***Wholesale selling price is the most important competitive factor for marketing branded footwear.***

Conversely, charging a wholesale price to retailers that is below the geographic market average enhances the attractiveness of your company's brand, especially in the eyes of price-conscious shoppers, and can lead to market share gains at competitors' expense. The deeper the price cuts, the greater the potential sales gains unless the effects of a lower price are negated by sub-par quality, comparatively few models/styles for buyers to choose among, insufficient advertising, the absence of celebrity endorsements, and a small network of retail outlets — ***low price alone is generally not sufficient for capturing a big market share***. Moreover, higher-priced rivals can offer customer rebates to dampen the market share losses to lower-priced rivals offering no rebates or smaller rebates.

In the private-label segment of the North American market, selling price is the decisive factor determining chain store purchases. Chain stores specify minimum quality standards and model variety for footwear-makers to meet and then buy strictly on the basis of which manufacturers bid the lowest prices. However, ***chain store buyers automatically reject the bids of companies whose offer price is NOT less than $2.50 below the average price that manufacturers are charging North American dealers for branded footwear***.

PRODUCT QUALITY. The quality of shoes produced at each plant is a function of four factors: (1) the percentage of long-wear materials used, (2) current-year expenditures for quality control per pair produced, (3) cumulative expenditures for quality control per pair produced (to reflect learning and experience curve effects), and (4) the amount spent per model for new features and styling. ***Efforts to boost quality by incorporating a progressively greater percentage of long-wear materials or by spending progressively greater amounts on quality control or new features and styling are subject to diminishing marginal benefits***. An independent association, the International Footwear Federation, obtains the needed data annually from all footwear plants, tests all models and brands on the market, and rates the quality of shoes produced at each plant of each company. The ratings of product quality at each plant range from a low of 0 to a high of 250; a rating of 50 denotes "minimal quality" and a rating of 100 is considered "satisfactory."

> ***The four factors that determine PRODUCT QUALITY are:***
> - ***Long-wear materials percentage***
> - ***Quality control expenditures per pair produced (in current year)***
> - ***Cumulative quality control expenditures per pair produced***
> - ***Styling/features budget per model***

The Federation's formula for calculating product quality at each plant is complex because of diminishing marginal benefits associated with greater expenditures and effort on each quality determinant, but the approximate composition of the rating points is as follows:

Quality Measure	Possible Number of Quality Rating Points
Percentage use of long-wear materials at each plant	0 – 90 points
Current-year quality control expenditures per pair produced at each plant	0 – 45 points
The company's overall average expenditure for quality control per pair produced at all plants for all years (this measures the extent of the company's long-term quality control effort and also allows for the transfer of quality know-how and effort across plants)	0 – 80 points
Styling/features expenditures per model at each plant	0 – 90 points

The sum of the points a plant gets on all four factors equals the plant's quality rating, subject to the 250-point limit. ***The Federation then takes the ratings of shoe quality at each plant and, based on where each plant's output is shipped and on the quality of pairs in unsold inventory, calculates quality ratings for each company in each market where its shoes are available for sale. Companies thus have four quality ratings—one for private-label shoes offered for sale in North America and one each for branded shoes offered for sale in North America, Europe, and Asia.*** A company's quality rating in each market segment is a ***weighted average*** of the product quality at the plants from which the pairs were shipped, adjusted up or down by the number and quality of any unsold pairs in inventory. For example, if a company had no unsold inventory in its European warehouse and it then shipped in 500,000 pairs from a plant with a production quality rating of 50 and 500,000 pairs from a plant with a production quality rating of 100, the company's weighted average quality rating for the 1,000,000 pairs available for sale in Europe would equal 75. ***The Federation's quality rating formula also reduces the quality rating on all unsold private-label pairs by 5 points and the quality ratings on all unsold branded pairs by 10 points carried over in inventory to the following year*** since they represent last year's models and styles.

The Federation's ratings of each company's shoe quality in each market segment are published annually in the Footwear Industry Report and often are the subject of newspaper and magazine articles. Market research confirms that many consumers are well-informed about the quality ratings and consider them in deciding which brand to buy. For example, if two competing brands were equally priced, most consumers would be inclined to buy the brand with the highest quality. ***Chain store accounts currently require a minimum quality rating of 50 on all private-label footwear purchased; the bids of manufacturers with quality ratings below 50 are automatically rejected.***

In Year 10, the footwear produced at the company's Ohio and Texas plants both carried a quality rating of 100, giving the company a quality rating of 100 in all three branded market segments. The company's private-label quality rating in Year 10 was 98 because there were 100,000 pairs of lower quality shoes left in private-label inventory from the previous year. It was prior management's policy to produce a fairly uniform quality shoe for all markets, but you and your co-managers have the authority to produce and market different quality shoes in different markets if you decide to do so. ***Other competitive factors being equal (price, service, advertising, and so on), companies with higher quality shoes will outsell companies with lower quality shoes.***

THE NUMBER OF RETAIL OUTLETS. Retail outlets are essential in accessing the consumer market. The more retail outlets a company has carrying its brand of shoes, the more market exposure a manufacturer has and the easier it is for consumers to purchase the brand. While having more retail outlets is generally better than having fewer outlets, a company can still generate substantial sales in a geographic area with as few as 100 retail outlets, provided the company's shoe line is otherwise amply attractive to consumers. Retailers, however, do not normally stock only one line of athletic footwear; most outlets carry 3 to 5 brands to provide customers with greater brand selection. It is very easy for a company to recruit more retailers to handle its brands because of the growing popularity of athletic footwear. At present, it costs $100 annually to support each retail outlet in a company's retail dealer network. This charge represents the costs of making sales calls, providing retailers with in-store promotional materials, printing catalogs showing models and prices, furnishing store clerks with sales information, and maintaining current credit ratings for each retailer. Currently, your company has 5000 North American retail outlets, 1000 European outlets, and 500 Asian outlets. ***If all other competitive factors are equal, companies with larger numbers of retail outlets in a given geographic area will outsell companies with smaller retail networks.***

SERVICE TO RETAILERS. Footwear retailers are inclined to push the brands of those footwear manufacturers that provide the best service. Customer service is a function of (1) actual delivery time achieved ***in the previous year*** on footwear orders, (2) whether distribution centers are staffed with enough customer service representatives to give retailer orders and inquiries timely, efficient attention, and (3) whether a manufacturer has stocked out of certain sizes and models ***in the previous year*** and been unable to fill retailer orders. The International Footwear Federation also calculates and reports service ratings for each manufacturer in each geographic market. Each company's customer service ratings for North America, Europe, and Asia are published annually in the Footwear Industry Report. Athletic footwear retailers use the service ratings in deciding how many pairs to order from a particular company.

> ***The three factors that determine SERVICE RATINGS are:***
> - ***The delivery time achieved in the previous year***
> - ***The ratio of retail outlets to customer service representatives***
> - ***Stockouts in the previous year***

As with the quality rating, the Federation's service rating ranges from a low of 0 to a high of 250. The Federation's formula for calculating service ratings is based on the following point system:

Service Measure		Service Rating Points
Delivery time achieved (in previous year)	4 weeks	0 points
	3 weeks	30 points
	2 weeks	65 points
	1 week	100 points
Number of retail outlets per customer service representative		–30 points to 80 points
Stockouts (in previous year)	under 100,000 pairs in a branded market	70 points
	over 100,000 pairs in a branded market	70 points down to –144 points depending on the size of the stockout as a percent of the company's branded sales in the region

While retailers can easily live with a 4-week delivery time on footwear orders, manufacturers can boost their service rating by cutting the delivery times to 3 weeks, 2 weeks, or 1 week. The Federation considers a ratio of 500 retail outlets per customer service representative "standard"; companies can boost their service ratings by maintaining an outlet-to-rep ratio under the 500-outlet-per-rep benchmark or can elect to economize on service costs by having a ratio greater than 500:1. Stockouts above 100,000 pairs reduce the service rating; the bigger the stockout percentage, the bigger the service rating penalty. ***The Federation's formula regarding stockouts calls for the maximum penalty of –144 points anytime a company's stockouts exceed 100% of branded sales*** (provided the stockout is greater than 100,000 pairs). The Federation believes a severe service rating penalty is justified for 100%-plus stockouts because stockouts of such magnitude mean that a company was unable to fill over half of its orders from retailers — an unacceptable condition from a retailer perspective. Since the sum of the points a company gets on all three service-related factors equals the rating for the year, the penalty for big stockouts is sizable enough to result in a zero customer service rating unless a company has a 1-week delivery time and a low retailer-to-rep ratio.

In Year 10, your company's service rating was 100 in all three geographic regions, determined as follows: 30 points for 3-week delivery, 0 points for having the "standard" 500:1 outlet-per-customer rep ratio in all three areas, and 70 points for not having stocked out in Year 9. A service rating of 50 denotes "minimal service" and a rating of 100 is considered "satisfactory." ***Other competitive factors being equal (price, quality, and so on), companies with higher service ratings will outsell companies with lower service ratings.***

CURRENT-YEAR ADVERTISING. Media advertising is used to inform the public of newly introduced models and styling and to tout the company's brand. Even though retail dealers act as an important information source for customers and actively push the brands they carry, advertising strengthens brand awareness, helps pull shoe buyers into retail stores carrying that brand, and informs people about the latest styles and models. The competitive impact of advertising depends on the size of .your company's current-year advertising budget. A company's market aggressiveness in promoting its lineup of models and styles in a given geographic area is judged stronger when its annual advertising expenditures ***exceed*** the area average and is judged weaker the further its ad budget is ***below*** what rival companies are spending on average. ***Other competitive factors being equal, companies with above-average current-year advertising expenditures will outsell companies with below-average current advertising expenditures.***

CELEBRITY ENDORSEMENTS AND BRAND IMAGE. As in other industries, footwear companies can contract with celebrity sports figures to endorse their footwear brand and appear in company ads. Celebrity endorsements, along with the impressions and perceptions people gain from watching a company's media ads over time, combine to define how strong a brand image a company enjoys in the minds of athletic footwear buyers. Studies confirm that ***a company's brand image has a significant effect on buyer purchases.***

Each year the International Footwear Federation conducts studies to determine each company's brand image and calculates an ***image rating*** for each company in each geographic region — North America, Europe, and Asia. The Federation's brand image rating is based on two factors: (1) the ***cumulative*** amount of advertising a company has done in a given geographic area over time and (2) the combined influence of a company's celebrity endorsers. ***Cumulative advertising has a 60% weight and celebrity endorsements have a 40% weight in the Federation's image rating formula.*** Company image ratings can range from a low of 0 to a high of 250. In effect, ***the company with the largest cumulative advertising in a geographic region and the most influential celebrity lineup enjoys the strongest brand image in that region.*** The stronger a company's brand image in a given geographic market relative to rival companies, the stronger is buyer loyalty and demand for the company's athletic footwear in that market.

> ***The two factors that determine IMAGE RATINGS are:***
> - ***Cumulative advertising expenditures (60%)***
> - ***Celebrity endorsements (40%)***

PRODUCT LINE BREADTH. Companies can elect to have a product line consisting of 50, 100, 150, 200, or 250 models or styles. To be regarded as a full-line producer, a company needs to have 250 models in its product line. A company with 50 models is looked upon as a specialty-line manufacturer. The competitive value of a broader product line is that the company can participate in more end-use segments (jogging, walking, aerobics, basketball, golf, tennis, and so on) and give customers a wider selection of shoe types and styles to choose from — in effect, the more models/styles a company has in its product line, the more consumers with reasons to consider buying one or more pairs of the company's footwear. ***Offering a wider product line and giving buyers more models/styles to choose from thus has a strong positive impact on a company's sales volume.*** If all other competitive factors are equal (price, quality, service, advertising, brand image, and so on), companies with more models and styles in their product lines will outsell companies offering fewer models.

Each plant is capable of producing 50, 100, 150, 200, or 250 models. The number of models a company has available in a given distribution center is a function of the number of models/styles produced at the plants from which the shoes were shipped. For example, if a company has 500,000 pairs of shoes available for sale in its Asian distribution center in Singapore and half of the pairs came from a plant producing 100 models and half came from a plant producing 200 models, then the weighted average number of models/styles that Asian consumers have to choose from is 150.

CUSTOMER REBATES. As an added sales inducement, manufacturers have the option of offering shoe buyers a rebate on each pair purchased from retailers. Some manufacturers offer promotional rebates and some don't. Rebates, if offered, can range from as low as $1 per pair to as much as $10 per pair. Manufacturers who give rebates provide retailers with rebate coupons to give buyers at the time of purchase. To obtain the rebate a customer must fill out the coupon and mail it to the manufacturer's distribution warehouse, along with the receipt of purchase. The customer service staff at the warehouse handles verification, check processing, and mailing the rebate. Some buyers lose the coupon and other buyers, for various reasons, fail to take advantage of the rebate offering. Studies show that 15% of purchasers mail in the $1 rebate coupons; 20% mail in the $2 coupon; 25% redeem the $3 coupon; and so on up to 60% for the $10 coupon. ***Other things being equal (price, quality, brand image, and so on), companies offering bigger rebates will outsell companies offering smaller rebates (or no rebates)***.

COMPETITIVE STRATEGY OPTIONS

With eight competitive weapons at your disposal, you and your co-managers have many strategic options for positioning your company in the global marketplace and trying to outcompete rival companies. You can put more or less emphasis than competitors on winning sales in North America or Europe or Asia. You can emphasize or de-emphasize private-label sales. In the branded market, you can pursue a competitive advantage keyed to low-cost/low-price, top-notch quality, superior service, brand name and brand image, a bigger network of retail outlets, a broader product line (up to 250 models), bigger promotional rebates, or any combination of these. You can pursue a similar competitive strategy in all three geographic markets or you can craft different strategies keyed to the different conditions prevailing in each geographic market. ***There's no built-in bias that favors any one strategy over all the others*** — most any well-conceived, well-executed competitive approach is capable of producing good financial performance, ***provided it is not overpowered by the strategies of your competitors***. Which company or companies win out in the upcoming battle for industry leadership will depend entirely on who is able to outstrategize, outcompete, and outperform the others.

Section 2

Company Operations and Reports

Your company began footwear manufacturing operations ten years ago in a converted two-story warehouse in Cincinnati using makeshift equipment. John Delgaudio, Richard Tebo, and Walter Ruggles — the three co-founders — developed a modestly innovative line of athletic footwear and then proceeded over the next ten years to transform their fledgling Ohio-based enterprise into an $83 million public company with budding opportunities in the global market for athletic-style shoes. The company has two plants — a 1,000,000 pair per year plant jammed into the cramped Cincinnati warehouse and a modern plant outside San Antonio that can turn out 2,000,000 pairs annually. Distribution warehouses have been opened in the United States (in Memphis, Tennessee), in Europe (Brussels, Belgium), and in Asia (Singapore) to serve the world's three biggest geographic markets. The company's stock price has risen from $5.00 in Year 7, when the company went public, to $15 at the end of Year 10. The stock is traded in the over-the-counter market (NASDAQ); there are 5,000,000 shares of the company's stock outstanding. Industry analysts believe the company is well-positioned for long-term growth and success provided the company's new management team can craft and execute a winning strategy.

Each year the company's corporate staff prepares eight concise reports reviewing the results of company operations. These include a manufacturing report, a warehouse and sales report, a marketing and administrative expense report, a geographic profit report, a cost report, an income statement, a year-end balance sheet, and a cash flow report. In addition, each year the company receives three different industry reports containing assorted industry statistics, details on the financial performance of all companies in the industry, a five-year forecast of footwear demand, plus a substantial amount of information about competitors (prices charged, pairs sold, quality and service ratings, advertising expenditures, celebrity endorsements, number of retail outlets, number of models, rebate programs, and image ratings). Guided by this information, you and your co-managers can respond to changing market and competitive conditions and modify your company's strategy for the upcoming year as needed.

The Manufacturing Report

The first of the set of eight company reports is the Manufacturing Report. The Manufacturing Report gives you a rundown of production operations — manufacturing costs, assorted manufacturing statistics, the amount invested in plant and equipment, and plant capacity information.

Table 2-1: Manufacturing Report, Year 10

		Ohio	Texas	Europe	Asia	Overall
Manufacturing Costs:						
Materials —	Normal-Wear	$3,600	$9,000	$0	$0	$12,600
	Long-Wear	2,400	6,000	0	0	8,400
Labor —	Annual Wages	5,120	8,004	0	0	13,124
	Incentive Pay	564	2,850	0	0	3,414
	Overtime Pay	0	0	0	0	0
Plant Supervision		1,600	3,335	0	0	4,935
Quality Control		315	785	0	0	1,100
Styling / Features		500	500	0	0	1,000
Production Methods		0	0	0	0	0
Production Run Set-Up		2,000	2,000	0	0	4,000
Plant Maintenance		1,006	1,890	0	0	2,896
Depreciation		875	1,890	0	0	2,756
Total Manufacturing Costs		$17,980	$36,254	$0	$0	$54,234
Manufacturing Statistics:						
Pairs Produced –	w/o Overtime	800	2,000	0	0	2,800
	with Overtime	0	0	0	0	0
Pairs Rejected		48	100	0	0	148
Net Production		752	1,900	0	0	2,652
Reject Percentage		6.00%	5.00%	0.00%	0.00%	5.29%
Quality of Pairs Produced		100	100	0	0	100
Work Force Statistics:						
Number of Workers Employed		320	667	0	0	987
Worker Productivity		2,500	3,000	0	0	2,838
Annual Wages Per Worker		$16.0	$12.0	$0.0	$0.0	$13.3
Incentive Pay Per Worker		1.8	4.3	0.0	0.0	3.5
Total Compensation		$17.8	$16.3	$0.0	$0.0	$16.8
Incentive Pay as % of Total		9.9%	26.3%	0.0%	0.0%	20.6%
Plant Investment:						
Gross Plant Investment		$17,500	$37,800	$0	$0	$55,300
Accumulated Depreciation		6,875	5,640	0	0	12,515
Net Plant Investment		$10,625	$32,160	$0	$0	$42,785
Plant Status:						
Year 10 Plant Capacity		1,000	2,000	0	0	3,000
New Plant Capacity			0	0	0	0
Expanded Plant Capacity			0	0	0	0
Capacity Purchased (Sold)			0	0	0	0
Y11 Capacity —	w/o Overtime	1,000	2,000	0	0	3,000
	with Overtime	1,200	2,400	0	0	3,600
Automation —	Ordered	-none-	-none-	-none-	-none-	
Options	On-Line	-none-	-none-	-none-	-none-	

The figures in Table 2-1 show the situation you are dealing with as you take over management of the company and prepare a strategy and set of decisions for Year 11. ***All figures in these and other reports are in thousands, except for the percentages and per pair items.*** The first section of the Manufacturing Report itemizes the manufacturing costs incurred at each plant, with an all-plant total in the last column. All the zeros in the columns for Europe and Asia reflect the fact that your company has not yet built plants in Europe or Asia and thus has nothing to report in these two areas.

MATERIALS COSTS. In Year 10, your company used a materials mix of 75% normal-wear and 25% long-wear to make 800,000 pairs at the Ohio plant and 2,000,000 pairs at the Texas plant. Prior management opted to use the same percentage mix of normal and long-wear materials at both the Ohio and Texas plants — you and your co-managers, however, have the latitude to use different percentages at different plants if you wish. The Year 10 price paid for normal-wear materials was $6 per pair produced; the price paid for long-wear materials was $12 per pair. Given the 75% - 25% mix, the materials costs at the Ohio plant were:

$$\text{Normal-wear materials: } \$6 \times 800{,}000 \text{ pairs} \times 0.75 = \$3{,}600{,}000$$

$$\text{Long-wear materials: } \$12 \times 800{,}000 \text{ pairs} \times 0.25 = \$2{,}400{,}000$$

You can verify Year 10's materials costs for the Texas plant in the same manner. While the Year 10 prices for normal-wear and long-wear materials were $6 and $12, respectively, material prices are subject to change if worldwide production capacity utilization falls below 90% or goes above 100% or if worldwide usage of long-wear materials exceeds 25%.

The company maintains no inventories of normal-wear and long-wear materials because suppliers have the capability to make deliveries on an as-needed basis. Plant managers provide suppliers with production schedules two weeks in advance to enable them to arrange for materials deliveries.

LABOR COSTS. Labor costs consist of base wages and fringe benefits, piecework incentives paid for each pair produced that meet quality standards, and overtime pay. In Year 10, labor costs totaled $5,684,000 at the Ohio plant and $10,854,000 at the Texas plant. Given production of 800,000 pairs in Ohio and 2,000,000 pairs in Texas, this is equivalent to labor costs per pair produced of $7.11 in Ohio ($5,684,000 ÷ 800,000 pairs = $7.105) and $5.43 in Texas ($10,854,000 ÷ 2,000,000 pairs = $5.427). The per pair labor cost differential between Ohio and Texas was attributable to differing wage rates, piecework incentives, and productivity levels. The labor compensation differences between Ohio and Texas reflect the availability of lower-wage labor at the Texas plant plus an attempt to put more emphasis on compensating Texas plant workers via piecework incentives.

Labor Cost Situation in Year 10	*Ohio Plant*	*Texas Plant*
Annual wages / fringes per worker	*$16,000*	*$12,000*
Piecework incentive paid for each pair meeting quality standards	*$0.75/pair*	*$1.50/pair*
Total annual incentive pay earned per worker	*$1,763*	*$4,275*
Number of workers employed	*320*	*667*
Total compensation per worker (wages plus piecework incentive)	*$17,763*	*$16,275*
Worker productivity (pairs per worker per year including rejects)	*2,500 pairs*	*3,000 pairs*
Labor cost per pair produced (including rejects)	*$7.11*	*$5.43*

Productivity at the Ohio plant has been a troublesome issue for the past five years, remaining well below the number of pairs produced per worker per year in Texas.[1] The lower

[1] *Overall worker productivity in a plant is calculated by dividing total pairs produced (without the use of overtime) by the number of workers employed to give the average number of pairs produced per worker per year.*

labor productivity in Ohio is partly attributable to obsolete equipment still being used in some sections of the Cincinnati plant and to inefficiencies in the plant layout. But some of the problem rests with prior management's policy of compensating Ohio plant workers via higher annual wages instead of higher incentive pay.

PRODUCTIVITY AND WORKER PAY. Worker productivity at each plant is affected by four things: (1) the ***percentage*** increase in the annual wage granted to workers each year, (2) how much emphasis is placed on incentive compensation (as measured by the percentage of the company's total compensation package accounted for by incentive pay), (3) how the company's total compensation package (annual wage plus total incentive pay before any overtime) compares against the average compensation package of other footwear companies with plants in the same geographic area, and (4) your expenditures for production methods improvements in each plant. Logically enough, the bigger the annual increase in the base wage, the bigger the boost to worker productivity. Wage increases in the 5-10% range can lead to productivity gains of as much as 6%; past a 12% annual base wage increase the productivity gain from higher wages depends solely on how much better your resulting compensation package is relative to other companies. To keep productivity rising year after year by means of wage payments, you and your co-managers will have to grant base wage increases each year.

> ***The four variables that affect WORKER PRODUCTIVITY are:***
> - ***The annual percentage increase in the base wage***
> - ***Incentive compensation as a percent of total compensation***
> - ***Company total compensation versus industry average total compensation***
> - ***Expenditures for production methods improvements (by plant)***

Pairs Produced Per Worker Per Year

	Ohio Plant	Texas Plant
Year 6	2,150	not open
Year 7	2,275	2,700
Year 8	2,360	2,800
Year 9	2,430	2,900
Year 10	2,500	3,000

Paying workers a piecework incentive motivates workers to exert greater on-the-job effort and produces a *continuing* boost to productivity year after year — ***a $1.50 per pair bonus incentive offered in Year 11 will motivate workers to produce more pairs in Year 11 and it will motivate them to achieve still higher productivity levels in Year 12, Year 13, and afterward even if the $1.50 incentive is not increased.*** The larger the percentage of workers' total compensation coming from piecework bonuses, the larger the *annual* boost to worker productivity. However, ***once incentive payments exceed 25% of total compensation, the annual percentage gain in productivity is subject to smaller and smaller marginal benefits; past 50% of total compensation, the gains in productivity attributable to higher incentive compensation fall to zero.*** In Year 10, incentive pay represented 9.9% of workers' total compensation in Ohio ($1,763 ÷ $17,763) and 26.3% of workers' total compensation in Texas ($4,275 ÷ $16,275).

When a company's total compensation package at a particular plant location is below the average of all other footwear companies having plants in the same geographic area, worker morale suffers, the plant will lose some of its best workers to better-paying rivals, and worker productivity at the plant is penalized. The bigger the compensation gap, the greater the adverse effect on productivity at that plant. Conversely, when a plant's workers are compensated at annual amounts *above* the geographic area average, worker productivity is greater than it otherwise would be because of the ability to attract and retain higher caliber workers. Consequently, you and your co-managers will need to consider the size of the annual wage increases you grant, the amount of incentive compensation being paid, and how well your workers are being compensated relative to workers at competing companies (pay comparisons are reported annually on page 9 of the Footwear Industry Report).

Both the Ohio and Texas plants are nonunion plants, and there presently is no threat of unionization at either location. Management has the authority to raise or lower both the annual wage component and the piecework incentive component of the compensation package. However, ***workers expect an increase in their annual wage each year***, and ***any cut in the annual wage will cause worker productivity to suffer***; the bigger the cut the larger the drop in productivity, other things remaining equal. A 10% base wage cut could result in a 7-15% falloff in productivity (depending on how competitive your overall compensation package turns out to be); a 20-30% base wage cut could lead to a 25 - 40% productivity penalty — again depending on the resulting competitiveness of your overall compensation package. Increases in incentive compensation, though, can restore ***some*** of the productivity loss from a reduction in the base wage.

> *Any cut in the annual base wage will cause worker productivity to suffer.*

The absolute minimum annual wage that can be paid at Texas and Ohio plants is $10,000; amounts below this put the company in violation of minimum wage laws. It has been the practice of prior management (the three co-founders) to make upward adjustments in the annual compensation package at both U.S. plants. Workers have thus come to expect either an increase in the annual base wage or the incentive bonus per pair or both.

Wage rates in Europe and Asia for workers of the type suitable for footwear production are lower than in the United States. If your company builds a European plant, workers can be employed for a base wage as low as $9,000 annually. Workers can be employed at Asian plants for as low as $2,500 annually. Higher annual wages at such plants may be paid at management's discretion. Piecework incentives can be used to ***supplement*** the minimum $9,000 and $2,500 annual wage packages in Europe and Asia but they cannot be used as a substitute for the payment of the $9,000 and $2,500 geographic minimums.

All overtime work in all geographic areas entails overtime labor costs equal to 1.5 times the normal base wage cost per pair produced; the prevailing piecework incentive bonus is also paid on all non-defective pairs produced at overtime in addition to the overtime wage. The figure which appears for overtime labor on line 5 of the manufacturing report always includes ***all*** overtime compensation — overtime wages plus the applicable incentive pay per pair at overtime. ***The number of pairs which can be produced at a plant without the use of overtime is limited to plant capacity or to the number of workers employed times productivity per worker, whichever is less.*** For instance, if you and your co-managers decide next year to employ 300 workers at the Ohio plant (instead of 320 as in Year 10), and if worker productivity continues to be 2,500 pairs per worker per year, then the maximum number of pairs which can be produced without use of overtime is 300 × 2,500 or 750,000 pairs; with a work force of 300 and productivity of 2,500 pairs, overtime production will thus begin at 750,000 pairs instead of 1,000,000 pairs. Moreover, the maximum amount which can be produced at overtime with 300 workers is 20% of 750,000 pairs or 150,000 pairs, not 200,000 pairs as would be the case if the plant were staffed to full production capacity. ***You and your co-managers will need to assess the economics of using overtime to increase production as opposed to hiring more workers (or building new capacity).***

Worker turnover rates at the company's manufacturing plants are not a significant labor cost consideration because of the comparative ease of hiring and training replacements. The company's personnel department maintains a list of qualified workers who can be put on the assembly line quickly when turnover occurs; most workers comply with the company's policy of giving two weeks notice before quitting.

PLANT SUPERVISION COSTS. Plant supervision costs at all plants currently amount to $5,000 per worker per year; this amount includes managerial and supervisory payroll costs and assorted plant overhead costs. As you can see from the Year 10 manufacturing report, supervision costs amounted to $1,600,000 in Ohio and $3,335,000 in Texas, reflecting employment of 320 and 667 workers, respectively. The $5,000 supervision cost per worker is subject to change as the game progresses.

QUALITY CONTROL EXPENDITURES AND REJECT RATES. Your company spent $315,000 on quality control in Ohio in Year 10 and $785,000 in Texas. The amount spent on quality control is important in two respects. The annual expenditure on QC at a given plant has a significant impact on the number of pairs which pass final inspection. The bigger the annual QC effort at a plant (measured in terms of QC expenditures per pair produced), the smaller the reject rate at final inspection. Second, the annual quality control expenditures at a plant and cumulative per pair expenditures companywide are two of the major components in the International Footwear Federation's annual quality rating calculation.

In Year 10, 48,000 of the 800,000 pairs produced at the Ohio plant failed final inspection, a reject rate of 6.0%. In Texas, 100,000 pairs were rejected, equal to a 5.0% reject rate. The reject rate at the Ohio plant has historically been high relative to the Texas plant:

Percentage of Production Rejected

	Ohio Plant	Texas Plant
Year 6	6.50%	not open
Year 7	6.75%	6.00%
Year 8	6.38%	5.66%
Year 9	5.80%	5.33%
Year 10	6.00%	5.00%

The reject rate at each plant is a function of (1) annual quality control expenditures per pair produced, (2) the size of the piecework incentive per pair produced, and (3) the number of different models in the company's product line. The "standard" reject rate is 6.0% at the Ohio plant and 5.0% at all other plants. ***Increasing annual QC expenditures per pair produced tends to reduce the reject rate below the standard. Raising the piecework incentive*** (say, from $1.00 to $1.25) ***also pulls the reject rates down*** because of increased worker attention to accurate workmanship. ***Workers are not paid a piecework bonus on pairs which fail final inspection***; this policy is a key part of the company's quality control strategy, since it motivates workers to watch the details of what they are doing and not take unwise shortcuts to boost their piecework output. ***Increasing the number of models produced causes the reject rate to rise; this is because of more frequent production run change-overs and reduced worker experience in making each model.*** It is long-standing company policy to donate all defective pairs to charitable organizations; thus, all pairs that fail final inspection represent deadweight cost and lost revenues.

> ***The three variables that affect plant REJECT RATES are:***
> - ***Annual quality control expenditures per pair produced***
> - ***The size of the piecework incentive per pair produced***
> - ***The number of different models in the year's production run.***

STYLING/FEATURES COSTS. The company maintains a staff of people who work exclusively on keeping the company's product line fresh and innovative. Once management decides how many models to produce at each plant (the options are 50, 100, 150, 200, or 250), this staff is charged with coming up with the needed footwear designs and styling/features for the company to promote each year. The caliber of their styles and designs is a function of the size budget they are given; the amount budgeted per model/style at each plant is used by the International Footwear Federation in calculating the plant's annual quality rating.

In Year 10, prior management decided to allocate $500,000 for the styling/features effort at each of the company's two plants. Management also decided to produce 100 models/styles in Ohio and 100 models/styles in Texas, resulting in average expenditures per model/style of $5,000 at each plant.

EXPENDITURES FOR PRODUCTION METHODS IMPROVEMENTS. Prior management began a program to improve production methods at both the Ohio and Texas plants. Outside consultants have determined that a long-term program to upgrade and reengineer manufacturing practices in the company's plants can reduce plant supervision costs by as much as 25% (in Year 10 plant supervision costs totaled $4,935,000), cut materials costs by as much as 25%, and increase annual worker productivity by as much as 500 pairs per worker per year. In Year 9, the company spent $350,000 on production methods improvements; $100,000 at the Ohio plant and $250,000 at the Texas plant. Even though company management was well-satisfied with the results of the effort, the program was temporarily discontinued in Year 10 in a budget-tightening effort to bolster Year 10's financial performance. Thus, as you can see in the cost sections of the Manufacturing Report for Year 10 (Table 2-1), no expenses are shown for production methods improvements.

You and your co-managers will have to decide whether to re-institute the effort to improve production methods. Spending for production methods improvements is one of the two best ways management has for achieving continuous reduction in production costs (the other is to achieve cost-efficient gains in worker productivity).

FIXED COSTS. Production run set-up costs vary according to the number of models produced at a plant. The annual set-up cost for 50 models is $1 million per plant; for 100 models it is $2 million per plant; for 150 models it is $3 million per plant, for 200 models it is $4 million per plant, and for 250 models it is $5 million. The size of the plant does not matter in determining production run set-up costs, only the number of models. Maintenance costs in a given year equal 5% of gross plant investment plus another 0.25% for each year of age past 5 years. The Texas plant, now four years old, had maintenance costs in Year 10 equal to 5% of its $37.8 million original cost, or $1,890,000; maintenance costs at the Texas plant will start climbing above $1,890,000 in Year 12 when the plant becomes 6 years old. The $1,006,000 maintenance cost for Ohio represented a 6.25% charge on the plant's original facilities (in operation for 10 years) and a 5.50% charge on the costs of maintaining the equipment added in Year 4. Plant life is 20 years and depreciation is calculated on a straight-line basis. Depreciation charges in Year 10 thus were $875,000 for the Ohio plant (5% of $17,500,000) and $1,890,000 for the Texas plant (5% of $37,800,000). The Ohio plant, while in operation for 10 years, is only 7 years old from a life-cycle standpoint because the whole plant's life was extended through Year 23 during the course of the expansion in Year 4.

Plant life is 20 years, and depreciation is calculated on a straight-line basis equal to 5% of gross plant investment per year.

PLANT INVESTMENTS. The fourth section of the Manufacturing Report keeps you posted on how much your company has invested in each plant. The amounts for "gross plant investment" represent the total dollar amounts the company has invested in each plant (initial plant costs, the capital cost associated with any expansion, plus any investment in automated equipment). The amounts shown for accumulated depreciation represent the combined depreciation charges for all years of plant operation. Net plant investment thus represents the undepreciated book value of the plant. Since all plant investments are treated as having a 20-year life and are depreciated on a straight-line basis, ***annual*** depreciation charges for a plant always equal 5% of gross plant investment.

PLANT CAPACITY. The plant status section shows current plant capacity and how much plant capacity your company will have on each continent in the upcoming year, given the plant construction, expansion, purchase, and sale decisions made previously. New plants can be built in Europe or Asia. Three plant sizes are available:

	Annual Capacity (with no overtime)	Annual Capacity (at full overtime)
Small Plant	1,000,000 pairs	1,200,000 pairs
Medium Plant	2,000,000 pairs	2,400,000 pairs
Large Plant	3,000,000 pairs	3,600,000 pairs

All plants regardless of size can be expanded, ***except for the Ohio plant***. Expansions must be in multiples of 1,000,000 pairs (1,000,000 or 2,000,000 or 3,000,000 and so on); ***there is a 9,000,000 pair limit on the size of plant expansion which can be undertaken at any one time at any one plant***. The Ohio plant is so space constrained that it cannot be expanded. Existing plants or parts of plants (in multiples of 1,000,000 pairs) can be purchased from or sold to another company in your industry. The prices are negotiated by the parties, but are subject to instructor/game administrator approval to ensure "arms-length" transactions. Transfer of ownership from seller to buyer occurs on January 1st of the year ***following*** the buy-sell approval.

> *No new plants can be built in North America; if additional North American plant capacity is needed, simply expand the Texas plant to achieve the same result. Only one new plant can be built in Europe and only one new plant can be constructed in Asia; if more European or Asian capacity is needed, expand the size of the plant already in operation to achieve the same result.*

AUTOMATION OPTIONS. The last two lines on the Manufacturing Report indicate whether a plant has automated equipment and provides a rundown on impending changes in plant capacity. You and your co-managers can improve a plant's manufacturing efficiency by investing in an ***automation option***. Three automation options are available for all plants. One involves using robotics to boost annual worker productivity by 500 pairs, one cuts the production run set-up costs by 40%, and a third results in a 25% cut in both production run set-up costs and plant supervision costs. A fourth productivity-boosting option is also available for the Texas and Ohio plants only. A detailed discussion of automation options is presented later in Section 3. So far, no automation option has been installed at the company's Ohio and Texas plants (as can be seen from the automation option item in the plant status section of Table 2-1).

THE WAREHOUSE AND SALES REPORT

Table 2-2 is a copy of your company's Year 10 Warehouse and Sales Report. All footwear produced at company plants is shipped directly to company-leased warehouses in Memphis, Brussels, and Singapore. Buyer orders are received, processed, and shipped from these warehouses on a schedule to meet the company's promised delivery time (1, 2, or 3, or 4 weeks). The pairs available at a particular warehouse can only be used to supply customers in the same geographic area as the warehouse. The more models offered for sale in a geographic region and the shorter the delivery time promised to retailers stocking the company's brand, the more inventory that has to be kept on hand in the warehouse to completely fill retailer orders for various sizes and styles. Insufficient inventory levels result in longer-than-promised delivery times. A ***stockout*** occurs whenever the total number of pairs ordered by area retailers exceed the pairs available at the area warehouse (beginning inventory plus incoming shipments from plants). Retailers whose orders cannot be filled will immediately place orders in the amount of the stockout with rival companies having pairs available. ***Stockouts reduce the company's service rating in the area the stockout occurs***. The larger the stockout (in percentage terms), the greater the service rating penalty.

from where to where to we ship dat products

Table 2-2: Warehouse and Sales Report, Year 10

	— North America — P-Label	Branded	Europe	Asia	Overall
Warehouse Operations:					
Beg. Footwear Inventory	100	3	2	0	105
Shipments from — Plants — Ohio	0	752	0	0	752
Texas	400	650	550	300	1,900
Europe	0	0	0	0	0
Asia	0	0	0	0	0
Pairs Available for Sale	500	1405	552	300	2,757
Pairs Sold	500	1250	500	240	2,490
Pairs Liquidated	0	0	0	0	0
Ending Footwear Inventory	0	155	52	60	267
Warehouse Stockouts (pairs)	0	0	0	0	0
Mfg. Cost of Goods Sold:					
Cost of Beginning Inventory	$1,984	$ 67	$ 40	$ 0	$ 2,091
+ Cost of Incoming Shipments	7,632	30,383	10,495	5,724	54,234
+ Exchange Rate Adjustment	0	0	(350)	(98)	(449)
– Cost of Ending Inventory	0	3,359	959	1,125	5,444
Mfg. Cost of Goods Sold	$9,616	$27,091	$ 9,225	$4,501	$50,433
Per Pair Sold	$19.23	$21.67	$18.45	$18.75	$20.25
Warehouse Expenses:					
Inventory Storage Charges	$ 25	$ 1	$ 0	$ 0	$ 26
Freight on Incoming Pairs	100	350	275	150	876
Import Tariffs	0	0	2,200	2,400	4,600
Warehouse Operations	921	2,304	1,100	580	4,905
Total Warehouse Exp.	$1,046	$2,655	$3,576	$3,130	$10,407
Per Pair Sold	$2.09	$2.12	$7.15	$13.04	$4.18
Impact of Exchange Rates on Cost of Pairs Shipped Into:					
P-Label — from Europe	$0				
from Asia	0				
N. A. — from Europe		$0			
from Asia		0			
Europe — from N. A.			$(350)		
from Asia			0		
Asia — from N. A.				$(98)	
from Europe				0	
Net Impact of Exch. Rates	$0	$0	$(350)	$(98)	$(449)
Per Pair Sold	$0.00	$0.00	$(0.70)	$(0.41)	$(0.18)

Manufacturing Costs of Goods Sold. The second section of the Warehouse and Sales Report provides manufacturing cost of goods sold information. As you know, it is standard accounting practice in income statements to base profit-and-loss determination on manufacturing cost of goods ***sold*** rather than on manufacturing cost of goods ***produced***. The two need not be equal. All pairs currently produced may not be sold (some pairs may be left over in inventory), in which case the total dollar value of manufacturing cost of goods produced (as shown in the manufacturing report) can exceed the total dollar value of manufacturing costs of goods sold (as shown in the warehouse and sales report). The reverse occurs when total number of pairs sold in a given year exceeds the number of pairs currently produced and beginning inventories are drawn down to supply the difference between the number sold and the number produced.

Manufacturing costs ***per pair sold*** were higher in the North American market in Year 10 because prior management shipped all production from the high-cost Ohio plant to the Memphis warehouse for sale as branded footwear in North America; the low cost Texas plant supplied all of the footwear sold in Europe, Asia, and the North American private-label market. A different pattern of shipment would have resulted in different costs and profit margins in each market. Note also that the cost of ending inventory is subtracted from the cost of pairs available to arrive at the total manufacturing cost of goods sold. The ending inventories in Year 10 are the company's beginning inventories in Year 11 and thus indicate what the company's inventory situation is as you and your co-managers take charge of operations for Year 11.

EXCHANGE RATE ADJUSTMENTS. This item in the manufacturing cost of goods sold section merits careful attention. Exchange rate adjustments result from the company's decision to sell its footwear in European and Asian countries. To handle the necessary foreign currency transactions and, also, to prepare for the possibility of constructing and operating plants in Europe and Asia, the company has established agreements with banks in the United States, Brussels, and Singapore to handle its various foreign currency transactions. The agreement covers payments the company receives from dealers in different countries, any currency exchanges arising out of the construction and operation of foreign plants should such occur in the future, and payments associated with importing or exporting footwear from area to area. The bank agreements call for all of the company's Asian transactions to be tied to the Japanese yen, all European transactions to be tied to the Eurodollar, and North American transactions to be tied to the U.S. dollar.

With help from the company's auditors (a prominent international accounting firm), the company has devised managerial accounting procedures to provide managers with information regarding the cost impact of exchange rate fluctuations between the dollar and the yen, the U.S. dollar and the Eurodollar, and the Eurodollar versus the yen. The company's simplified procedure calls for (1) manufacturing costs on footwear shipped between North America and Asia to be adjusted up or down for exchange rate changes between the U.S. dollar and the Japanese yen, (2) manufacturing costs on pairs shipped between North America and Europe to be adjusted up or down based on exchange rate fluctuations between the U.S. dollar and the Eurodollar, and (3) manufacturing costs on pairs shipped between Asia and Europe to be adjusted for fluctuations between the Eurodollar and the yen. No exchange rate adjustments are made on footwear shipments within geographic areas (from the Ohio and Texas plants to the Memphis distribution centers, from Asian plants to the Singapore distribution center, or from European plants to the Brussels distribution center) because operations within the same trade area are not impacted by fluctuating exchange rates.

> ***Fluctuations in EXCHANGE RATES increase or decrease the manufacturing cost of footwear shipped between geographic regions of the world. Exchange rate cost adjustments are calculated and accounted for automatically in the Warehouse and Sales Report.***

You and your co-managers can track movements in the value of the U.S. dollar against the Eurodollar and yen in *The Wall Street Journal* (usually page C-1), *USA Today*, and many local newspapers (your instructor/game administrator will inform you about how exchange rate fluctuations will be handled). As you may recall from your earlier studies of exchange rates, when the exchange rate of Japanese yen for U.S. dollars goes down (say from 104.80 yen per dollar to 104.45 yen per dollar), it takes fewer Japanese yen to purchase a U.S. dollar (or, conversely, $1 will exchange for fewer yen). Such an exchange rate change represents a ***decline*** in the value of the U.S. dollar and ***rise*** in the value of the Japanese yen. Insofar as your company's footwear business is concerned, a decline in the value of the dollar against the yen makes U.S.-made footwear more competitive in Asia — it takes fewer yen for Asian footwear retailers and consumers to buy U.S.-made shoes when the exchange rate is 100 yen per dollar than when the exchange rate is 105 yen per dollar.

The following statements sum up the effect of fluctuating exchange rates on producing footwear in one geographic area and exporting it for sale in another geographic market:

- A ***decline*** in the exchange rate of Japanese yen for U.S. dollars enhances the attractiveness of exporting goods from U.S. plants to Asian markets and reduces the attractiveness of producing goods in Asian plants for export to North American markets. Conversely, a ***rise*** in the exchange rate of yen for dollars reduces the attractiveness of exporting U.S.-made goods to Asia and enhances the attractiveness of exporting Asian-made goods to North America.
- A ***decline*** in the exchange rate of Eurodollars for U.S. dollars enhances the attractiveness of exporting goods from U.S. plants to European markets and reduces the attractiveness of producing goods in European plants for export to North American markets. Conversely, a ***rise*** in the exchange rate of Eurodollars for U.S. dollars reduces the attractiveness of exporting U.S.-made goods to Europe and enhances the attractiveness of exporting European-made goods to North America.
- A ***decline*** in the exchange rate of Japanese yen for Eurodollars enhances the attractiveness of exporting goods from European plants to Asian markets and reduces the attractiveness of producing goods in Asian plants for export to Europe. Conversely, a ***rise*** in the exchange rate of yen for Euros reduces the attractiveness of exporting European-made goods to Asia and enhances the attractiveness of exporting Asian-made goods to Europe.

> ***NOTE:*** *If the exchange rate of Japanese yen for Eurodollars is not published in the news source you have, you can easily calculate it by dividing the published quote for Japanese yen per U.S. dollar by the quoted exchange rate of Eurodollars per U.S. dollar. The computer does all the exchange rate calculations for you, however.*

As you might expect, the ins and outs of financial accounting for exchange rate fluctuations in a multinational company become rather complex. To make it easy for you and your co-managers to assess the competitive impact of fluctuating exchange rates on shipping goods produced in one geographic area to distribution centers in another geographic area, company accountants adjust the manufacturing cost of imported footwear upward or downward for the effects of exchange rate fluctuations. Positive numbers for the exchange rate adjustment in the manufacturing cost of goods sold section of the warehouse and sales report reflect an upward cost shift due to competitively adverse exchange rate movements; negative numbers reflect downward cost adjustments and competitively favorable exchange rate shifts.

In effect, the company bears the risk of exchange rate fluctuations. While other currency exchange arrangements could conceivably have been made, an analysis over the years shows that the risk is tolerable. The company's board of directors has decided that the present bank agreements and internal accounting practices concerning foreign exchange transactions will be continued indefinitely.[2] However, you and your co-managers can reduce the company's future exposure to adverse exchange rate fluctuations either (1) by building an Asian plant to serve the Asian market and a European plant to serve the European market, thereby reducing footwear shipments *across* geographic markets and reducing the cost impact of changing

---

[2]Adjusting manufacturing costs upward/downward in this fashion is a way of approximating the profit impact of fluctuating exchange rates. Strict adherence to financial accounting principles would require adjusting the company's selling prices and revenues instead of costs, but this would have made pricing decisions and price comparisons across companies much harder to interpret. So we opted to use a simplified approach for managerial reporting purposes and avoid the financial accounting intricacies associated with foreign currency transactions. We think you will appreciate the straightforward approach we've taken; it makes decision-making easier and approximates closely enough the competitive effects that exchange rate fluctuations have on companies doing business in global markets.

exchange rates or (2) by raising/lowering the amounts exported/imported on an annual basis, depending on whether current year exchange rate fluctuations are favorable/unfavorable.

As you can see from Table 2-2, in Year 10 the company had a favorable (negative) exchange rate adjustment of $350,000 on the 550,000 pairs of footwear exported to Europe and a favorable (negative) exchange rate adjustment of $98,000 on the 300,000 pairs exported from the Texas plant to Asia. The –$350,000 figure was derived from the following data:

	Exchange Rates of Eurodollars per U.S. Dollar	Manufacturing Cost of Pairs Produced in Texas and Shipped to Europe
End of Year 9	1.1689	
End of Year 10	1.1650	$10,495,000

The percentage change in the exchange rate of Eurodollars per U.S. dollar used to calculate the *annual* exchange rate adjustment is adjusted upward by a factor equal to 10 times the actual reported period-to-period percentage change. Multiplying the period-to-period change by a factor of 10 is done as a way of converting the effect of actual exchange rate movements over a period of several days (the interval between your decisions) into a change that represents a full year — the interval over which your company has produced and shipped footwear since the last report. The Year 10 percentage change in the exchange rate of Eurodollars for U.S. dollars, including the factor of 10 adjustment, was calculated thusly:

$$\frac{\text{Year 10} - \text{Year 9}}{\text{Year 9}} \times 10 = \frac{1.1650 - 1.1689}{1.1689} \times 10 = -0.03336 \text{ or } -3.336\%.$$

Applying this percentage change to the $10,495,000 value of U.S.-made goods exported to Europe gives:

$$-3.336\% \times \$10,495,000 = -\$350,163$$ (or –$350,000 rounded to the nearest thousand).[3]

The favorable or negative exchange rate adjustment of $98,000 on Year 10 footwear shipments to Singapore (shown in Table 2-2) is arrived at in similar fashion. The change in the yen from 104.98 in Year 9 to 104.80 in Year 10 works out to be –1.71%, which multiplied by shipments of $5,724,000, yields a favorable adjustment of –$98,000 (rounded to the nearest thousand).

> ***REMEMBER: A positive number for the exchange rate adjustment represents higher costs while a negative number represents lower costs. Should your company build plants in Europe and Asia, you can track the impact of exchange rate movements on the cost of footwear shipped from each geographic area where the company has plants by consulting the bottom section of the Warehouse and Sales Report.***

As the game progresses, don't be surprised if exchange rate fluctuations have a bearing on where it is most advantageous to locate plants, which plants to export from, and which geographic regions to export to. The bigger the changes in the exchange rates between these three currencies, the more company profitability is affected by how many pairs are exported from which plants to which geographic regions.

WAREHOUSE EXPENSES. The third section of the Warehouse and Sales Report contains a breakdown of warehouse-related expenses. The first warehouse expense component is inventory storage charges, currently pegged at $0.25 per pair. Storage charges in a given year

[3] *As you have noted by now, since most of the dollar figures are reported in thousands, rounding to the nearest thousand is standard procedure and accounts for why some of the figures reported are not exact down to the last dollar. Be assured, though, that the rounding "errors" have no material impact on the accounting accuracy of the information presented in the reports. Indeed, we think you will find that having the numbers rounded off to thousands is a welcome simplification.*

are based on the number of pairs carried over from the previous year — that is, the amount in beginning inventory. In Year 10 in the North American private-label segment, for example, the beginning inventory of 100,000 pairs resulted in a $25,000 inventory charge (100,000 pairs × $0.25 per pair). The inventory storage charge of $0.25 per pair becomes progressively larger at each warehouse as the size of unsold inventory rises. Inventory storage costs at ***each*** warehouse rise in stair-step fashion as the number of unsold pairs carried over to the next year rise. Storage costs are $0.25 per pair for the first 500,000 pairs in unsold inventory carried over from one year to the next; $0.50 for each of the next 250,000 pairs that are carried over; $0.75 per pair on each pair between 750,000 and 1,000,000 pairs; $1.00 on each pair between 1,000,000 and 1,250,000 pairs; and $1.50 on all pairs in excess of 1,250,000 pairs.

Currently it costs $0.25 per pair to ship footwear from a plant to a warehouse in the ***same*** geographic area and $0.50 per pair to ship footwear overseas to a ***different*** geographic area. Thus, the Year 10 charges of $150,000 for freight on incoming shipments to Asia shown in column 4 of Table 2-2 represent the cost of shipping 300,000 pairs at $0.50 per pair from Texas to Singapore.

Countries in both the European and Asian markets have imposed tariffs on imported footwear. Tariffs into the European market currently average $4 per pair and tariffs into Asia currently average $8 per pair. One reason to locate plants in Europe and Asia is to escape tariffs on footwear sold in these geographic markets. ***All tariffs are paid at the port of entry at the time of shipment even if the goods shipped in remain in the warehouse unsold.*** Tariff payments in Year 10 totaled $2,200,000 on shipments to Europe ($4 × 550,000 pairs) and $2,400,000 on shipments to Asia ($8 × 300,000 pairs).

North American governments (the U.S., Canada, and Mexico), believing in the economic benefits of free trade and open markets, do not currently impose tariffs on imported footwear. U.S. officials have talked to European and Asian governments about reducing the tariffs on North American-made footwear but there is no success to report at this point; discussions will continue. U.S. footwear companies have, in years past, lobbied Congress to impose tariffs and import quotas on European and Asian goods in retaliation, but no legislation is currently pending. As the game progresses, ***import tariffs in all markets are subject to change.*** But it is unlikely that tariffs will change without advance warning. Should there be any political developments to alter the present tariff structure, they will likely be reported in the Footwear Industry Report or announced by your instructor/game administrator.

Warehouse operating costs consist of (1) $100,000 in annual leasing fees for each distribution center facility and (2) a boxing, packing, and freight charge on each pair sold to retailers. All three company warehouses (Memphis, Brussels, Singapore) have been leased for 20 years; the $100,000 leasing fee must be paid even if the company later abandons the market (but the 20-year lease also protects the company's ability to re-enter a geographic market, and the $100,000 cost is modest). Each warehouse has sufficient capability to pack and ship whatever order volume can be generated from retailers. Warehouse crews are employed to box the shoes, label the boxes, and pack retailer orders into cartons for shipment. Company accountants have analyzed warehouse activities and found that there are scale economies in each warehouse's order-filling process. Labor, materials and equipment, and freight costs average $2 per pair on the first million pairs, $1.50 per pair on the next 2 million pairs, and $1 per pair on all shipments from the same warehouse in excess of 3 million pairs annually. The $1,100,000 cost of European warehouse operations in Year 10 (see column 3 in Table 2-2) represents $100,000 in leasing fees and $1,000,000 in labor, packaging materials, and freight charges ($2 per pair for each of the 500,000 pairs sold and shipped to European footwear

> ***All three company warehouses (Memphis, Brussels, Singapore) have been leased for 20 years, and the $100,000 annual leasing fee must be paid even if the company later abandons the geographic region.***

retailers in Year 10). Since the Memphis distribution warehouse ships both branded and private-label shoes, the down-stepping of order-filling costs is based on the combined volumes. The $100,000 lease cost for the Memphis warehouse is divided between private-label and branded costs based on the percentage of pairs shipped to each market segment.

THE MARKETING AND ADMINISTRATIVE REPORT

Table 2-3 shows the Year 10 Marketing and Administrative Report. It costs the company $100 in retailer support services for each outlet handling the company's brands. The retailer support costs shown in Table 2-3 represent Year 10 costs for 5000 North American outlets, 1000 European outlets, and 500 Asian outlets. Prior management spent $2,000,000 on North American advertising, $1,000,000 on advertising in Europe, and $500,000 on advertising to launch entry into several Asian countries. To help stimulate branded sales in Year 10, the company instituted rebate incentives — $3 rebates in North America, $2 rebates in Europe, and a $1 rebate in Asia. In North America, 25% of shoe buyers redeemed the $3 rebate coupons, creating redemption costs of $938,000 ($3 × 25% participation × 1,250,000 pairs sold).[4] In Europe, redemption costs were $200,000 ($2 × 20% participation × 500,000 pairs sold). There were $36,000 in redemption costs in Asia ($1 × 15% participation × 240,000 pairs sold). This was the first time the company used rebates.

Table 2-3: MARKETING AND ADMINISTRATIVE REPORT, YEAR 10

	North America	Europe	Asia	Overall
Marketing Expenses:				
Retailer Support Cost	$ 500	$ 100	$ 0	$ 650
Advertising Expenditures	2,000	1,000	500	3,500
Customer Rebates	938	200	36	1,174
Customer Service Staff	200	40	20	260
Cost of On-Time Delivery	312	125	60	498
Celebrity Endorsement Expenses	0	0	0	0
Total Marketing Expenses	$3,950	$1,465	$666	$6,081
Per Pair Sold	$3.16	$2.93	$2.77	$3.06
Administrative Expenses:				
Executive Salaries				$ 500
Other Corporate Overhead				2,000
Total Administrative Expenses				$2,500
Per Pair Sold				$1.00

The costs for customer service staff of $200,000 in the U.S., $40,000 in Europe and $20,000 in Asia reflect the costs of maintaining 10 customer service representatives in the Memphis warehouse, 2 in Brussels, and 1 in Singapore. In Year 10 the company spent an average of $20,000 annually for salaries, fringe benefits, office facilities, telephone charges, computer support, and office supplies for each customer service representative. Company accountants have just done a study indicating that the cost per customer service representative will escalate at the rate of 6% annually; thus, you can expect a cost of $21,200 per representative in Year 11, a cost of $22,472 in Year 12, and so on.

Costs for faster delivery arise out of managerial decisions to accelerate delivery of customer orders for branded shoes from the 4-week standard (the costs of which are included in

[4]*Since all customers do not bother to obtain the rebates, redemption costs are less than the face value of the coupons. The rebate redemption rates are listed on page 60 of this manual.*

the order-filling charge) to 3 weeks, 2 weeks, or 1 week. Shorter delivery times enhance the company's service rating. The cost to achieve 3-week delivery is currently $0.25 per pair; the cost of 2-week delivery is $0.75 per pair, and 1-week delivery costs $1.50 per pair. The Year 10 delivery charges reflect 3-week delivery in North America, Europe, and Asia. The per pair costs for faster delivery are subject to change as the game progresses. Chain store purchasing practices for private-label shoes permit 4-week delivery — shorter delivery times offer no value-added benefit.

ADMINISTRATIVE EXPENSES. The company has two categories of administrative expenses: executive salaries and corporate overhead (not including interest expenses). Executive salaries totaled $500,000 in Year 10 and will increase 5% annually beginning in Year 11. Corporate overhead represents the costs incurred for accounting, computer operations, headquarters office space and supplies, travel and entertainment, the subscription to the Footwear Industry Report, legal fees, corporate sales and marketing expenses, and assorted other companywide costs.

Corporate overhead increases as the company's production capacity (not including overtime) increases. The incremental overhead cost increases get progressively bigger, rising $750,000 for each 1,000,000 pairs of capacity up to a total of 5,000,000 pairs, by $1,000,000 for each of the next 2,000,000 pairs (up to a capacity of 7,000,000 pairs), by $1,500,000 for each of the next 3,000,000 pairs (up to a total capacity of 10,000,000 pairs), and by $2,000,000 for each million pairs of capacity over 10,000,000 pairs. Overhead will be reduced when capacity is sold or permanently shut down, but can never fall below the Year 10 base of $2,000,000.

THE GEOGRAPHIC PROFIT REPORT

The Year 10 Geographic Profit Report is presented in Table 2-4. Its purpose is to keep you informed about the company's profitability in the various geographic markets — which segments are more profitable and which are less profitable (or maybe even losing money). It shows the company's wholesale selling prices, per pair operating costs by category (manufacturing, distribution, marketing, and administration), and operating profits per pair for each geographic market. The per pair operating cost figures for manufacturing cost of goods sold and for distribution costs come from the Warehouse and Sales report. The marketing and administrative costs per pair sold come from the Marketing and Administrative report. Administrative costs per pair sold are always the same value across the three areas because the company's accounting methodology allocates the costs of headquarters' operations to each geographic area based upon the area's percentage of total pairs sold. Hence, if the breakdown of pairs sold is 75% in North America, 20% in Europe, and 5% in Asia, then companywide administrative costs are allocated in the same proportion.

As you can see from Table 2-4, operating profit per pair in Year 10 was highest in North America, and the company barely made money on the pairs sold in Asia. Profit per branded pair sold in North America was higher than in Europe or Asia mainly because the $1 higher price in Europe and the $2 higher price in Asia was not enough to cover higher costs associated with the $4 tariff on European imports and the $8 tariff on Asia imports. The differences in manufacturing costs across the four market segments reflect (1) the differences in production costs at the Ohio and Texas plants — the output of the Ohio plant was all used to supply branded demand in North America and (2) the effects of exchange rates on shoes shipped from Texas to Europe (a favorable adjustment of $350,000) and to Asia (a

> ***One reason for the attractively high operating profit per pair sold on private-label sales in Year 10 is because there are no marketing costs associated with selling to private-label buyers — sales are made solely on the basis of a low bid price.***

favorable adjustment of $98,000). Interest expenses are allocated to each geographic area based on the percentage of pairs sold. Observe that net profit per pair sold in Asia was negative in Year 10.

Table 2-4: GEOGRAPHIC PROFIT REPORT, YEAR 10

	— North America —				
	P-Label	**Branded**	**Europe**	**Asia**	**Overall**
Revenue-Cost-Profit Analysis Per Pair Sold:					
Sales Revenues	$28.34	$34.00	$35.00	$36.00	$33.26
Operating Costs — Manufacturing	19.23	21.67	18.45	18.75	20.25
Distribution	2.09	2.12	7.15	13.04	4.18
Marketing	0.00	3.16	2.93	2.77	2.44
Administrative	1.00	1.00	1.00	1.00	1.00
Operating Profit	6.01	6.04	5.47	0.43	5.38
Extraordinary Gain (Loss)	0.00	0.00	0.00	0.00	0.00
Interest Income (Expense)	(1.09)	(1.09)	(1.09)	(1.09)	(1.09)
Pre-Tax Profit	4.93	4.95	4.38	(0.66)	4.29
Income Taxes	1.48	1.49	1.31	(0.20)	1.29
Net Profit	$3.45	$3.47	$3.07	$(0.46)	$3.00
Inventory Liquidation Option:					
Liquidation Price	$0.00	$0.00	$0.00	$0.00	$0.00
Assigned Cost[1]	0.00	0.00	0.00	0.00	0.00
Pre-Tax Impact	$0.00	$0.00	$0.00	$0.00	$0.00
Total Pre-Tax Impact	$0	$0	$0	$0	$0
Expected Annual Cost Savings[2]	$0	$0	$0	$0	$0

[1] The cost per liquidated pair is the same as the manufacturing cost per pair sold through normal private-label or branded channels. Liquidated pairs are not assigned any warehouse, administrative, or interest costs.

[2] The expected cost savings is an estimate of the storage and finance costs that will be avoided annually.

Should you invoke the Inventory Liquidation Option, the bottom section of the Geographic Profit Report will display statistics concerning the revenue-cost-profit impact of liquidating excess inventories and an estimate of the savings realized next year because of reduced storage and inventory financing charges.

THE COST REPORT

The company's Year 10 Cost Report is shown in Table 2-5. It contains a breakdown of manufacturing costs per pair produced at each plant and itemized operating costs per pair sold in all four market segments. The Cost Report is especially valuable in comparing plant efficiency, tracking which costs are rising and falling as the game progresses, and monitoring the cost differences across market segments. You will find the information in this report essential in managing the company's operations, crafting a cost-effective strategy, and deciding what prices to charge.

As you can see from Table 2-5, in Year 10 manufacturing costs per pair produced at the company's Ohio plant were $23.91 versus costs of $19.08 at the Texas plant. Material costs at both plants were equal ($7.50 per pair produced) because in Year 10 prior management opted to use the same proportion of normal-wear and long-wear materials at both plants and paid the same prices for these materials at both plants.[5] The single biggest reason for the cost gap

[5] *In future years if you and your co-managers decide to use a different materials mix at different plants, then material costs will vary from plant to plant.*

between the Ohio and Texas plants in Year 10 was labor costs. Workers at the Ohio plant were paid $17,763 in wages and incentive pay and produced 2,500 pairs per worker — as shown in the Manufacturing Report in Table 2-1, giving rise to labor costs of $7.11 per pair produced ($17,763 ÷ 2,500). Workers at the Texas plant were paid $16,275 in wages and incentive pay and produced 3,000 pairs per worker, equal to labor costs of $5.71 per pair.

Table 2-5: Cost Report, Year 10

	Ohio	Texas	Europe	Asia	Overall
Costs Per Pair Produced:					
Materials	$ 7.50	$ 7.50	$ 0.00	$ 0.00	$ 7.50
Labor	7.11	5.43	0.00	0.00	5.91
Plant Supervision	2.00	1.67	0.00	0.00	1.76
Quality Control	0.39	0.39	0.00	0.00	0.39
Styling / Features	0.62	0.25	0.00	0.00	0.36
Production Methods	0.00	0.00	0.00	0.00	0
Waste due to Rejects	1.43	0.95	0.00	0.00	1.08
Production Run Set-Up	2.50	1.00	0.00	0.00	1.43
Plant Maintenance	1.26	0.94	0.00	0.00	1.03
Depreciation	1.09	0.94	0.00	0.00	0.99
Total Production Costs[1]	$23.91	$19.08	$0.00	$0.00	$20.45

	– North America –				
	P-Label	Branded	Europe	Asia	Overall
Costs Per Pair Sold:					
Production Costs	$19.23	$21.67	$19.08	$19.08	$20.43
Exchange Rate Adjustment	0.00	0.00	(0.63)	(0.33)	(0.18)
Inventory Cost Adjustment[2]	0.00	0.00	0.00	0.00	0.00
Mfg. Cost of Goods Sold	19.23	21.67	18.45	18.75	20.25
Warehouse Costs — Inventory Storage	0.05	0.00	0.00	0.00	0.01
Shipping Costs	0.20	0.28	0.55	0.62	0.35
Import Tariffs	0.00	0.00	4.40	10.00	1.85
Whse. Operations	1.84	1.84	2.20	2.42	1.97
Marketing Costs — Retailer Support	0.00	0.40	0.20	0.21	0.26
Advertising	0.00	1.60	2.00	2.08	1.41
Customer Rebates	0.00	0.75	0.40	0.15	0.47
Service Staff	0.00	0.16	0.08	0.08	0.10
On-Time Delivery	0.00	0.25	0.25	0.25	0.20
Celebrity Endorse.	0.00	0.00	0.00	0.00	0.00
Administrative Expenses	1.00	1.00	1.00	1.00	1.00
Interest Expense (Income)	1.09	1.09	1.09	1.09	1.09
Total Cost Per Pair Sold	$23.41	$29.05	$30.62	$36.66	$28.96

[1] Based on net production (after adjusting total pairs produced downward by the number of pairs rejected).

[2] The inventory cost adjustment represents the difference between the weighted average cost of pairs shipped and the weighted average cost of pairs held in inventory from the prior year. A negative number means that production costs (adjusted for exchange rates) were ABOVE the cost of pairs in beginning inventory. A positive number means that production costs were BELOW the cost of pairs in beginning inventory.

Supervisory costs per pair produced in Ohio were greater than in Texas because lower worker productivity in Ohio entailed the use of 320 workers (instead of the 267 workers that would have been needed had worker productivity in Ohio matched that in Texas). Plant supervision costs are $5,000 per worker, so economizing on the number of workers employed (via efforts to boost worker productivity and through use of overtime) holds down supervisory costs.

The Cost Report also shows that the company spent $0.39 per pair on quality control in both Ohio and Texas. Even though the company spent $500,000 on styling and features at each plant, the cost per pair produced in Ohio was higher than in Texas because of the Ohio plant's smaller production (800,000 pairs versus 2,000,000 pairs in Texas — see the Manufacturing Report in Table 2-1). The cost of pairs rejected in Ohio averaged $1.43 per salable pair versus $0.95 in Texas because of the Ohio plant's higher reject rate (6% versus 5%.). Production run set-up costs for the company's 100 models averaged $2.50 in Ohio ($2,000,000 ÷ 800,000 pairs) but only $1.00 in Texas ($2,000,000 ÷ 2,000,000 pairs), a reflection of scale economies — large plants can spread out the fixed production run set-up charges over more pairs.

Plant maintenance in Ohio ran $0.32 per pair more than in Texas because of the difference in plant age (the maintenance cost percentage is higher at older plants) and because the Ohio plant only operated at 80% of full capacity. Depreciation costs per salable pair were $0.15 per pair higher than in Texas because the Ohio plant operated at 80% of capacity while Texas operated at 100%. Had the Ohio plant operated at 100% of capacity, maintenance and depreciation charges would have averaged about $0.50 per pair less since the fixed maintenance and depreciation costs of $1,875,000 could have been spread over 1,000,000 pairs instead of just 800,000 pairs. You and your co-managers will undoubtedly want to explore ways to bring per pair costs in Ohio down more in line with those at the Texas plant.

The remainder of this report details the costs per pair sold in the private-label market and in each geographic market. The production costs per pair of $19.23 for private-label shoes and $19.08 for branded shoes in Europe and Asia are below the $21.67 branded cost in North America because all shipments to Europe and Asia and to the private-label segment were from the company's lower-cost Texas plant. Observe that exchange rate adjustments in Year 10 favorably impacted the company's cost per pair by $0.63 in Europe and by $0.33 in Asia.

The sum of current production costs per pair, the exchange rate adjustment, and the inventory cost adjustment equals the per pair manufacturing costs of goods sold. In Year 10, manufacturing costs per pair sold differed significantly across the three geographic markets — from a low of $18.45 in Europe to a high of $21.67 in the North American branded segment.

Warehouse expenses per pair sold are derived by dividing each of the total dollar amounts shown in the third section of the warehouse and sales report (see Table 2-2) by the number of pairs the company sold in each geographic market. Thus, even though the per pair shipping charges are $0.50 on shipments between North America and Asia, the average shipping cost of $0.62 for Asia arises because only 240,000 of the 300,000 pairs shipped to Asia in Year 10 were sold. The total freight charges of $150,000 on shipments to Asia were allocated to the 240,000 pairs sold ($150,000 ÷ 240,000 = $0.625). For the same reason, shipping charges to Europe averaged $0.55 per pair sold (instead of $0.50 had all the pairs shipped to Europe in Year 10 been sold) and tariffs on European sales averaged $4.40 per pair (instead of $4.00).

> ***It is standard accounting practice at your company to charge all operating costs incurred in a given year to the pairs sold in that year.***

As you can see from studying the composition of warehouse expenses for Year 10, the import tariffs imposed by European and Asian governments give rise to big differences in per pair warehouse costs for branded shoes across the three geographic regions. In addition, though, the small volumes sold through the Singapore warehouse caused the cost of warehouse operations in Asia to average $2.42 per pair ($580,000 ÷ 240,000 pairs sold) versus $2.20 in Europe and $1.84 in the United States. In Asia the $100,000 in fixed leasing costs for distribution facilities was spread over sales of just 240,000 pairs ($0.43 per pair) as compared to sales of 500,000 pairs in Europe ($0.20 per pair) and sales of 1,750,000 pairs in North America ($0.06 per pair) — a reflection of scale economies. In North America, the order-filling component of warehouse costs averaged only $1.78, compared to $2.00 in Europe and Asia, because warehouse volume in North America exceeded 1 million pairs (order-filling costs were only $1.50 per pair on last 750,000 pairs shipped) — also reflecting scale economies.

Marketing costs per pair sold are calculated by dividing expenditures for each marketing variable shown in the marketing and administrative report (see Table 2-4) by the number of pairs the company sold in each area. All marketing costs in North America are allocated to branded sales because no such expenses are needed to win private-label sales. In Year 10 the company's single biggest marketing cost for branded sales was advertising. Advertising costs in North America averaged $1.60 per pair sold (obtained by dividing the $2,000,000 the company spent on North American advertising by total North American sales of 1,250,000 branded pairs); advertising costs averaged $2.00 per pair sold in Europe and $2.08 per pair sold in Asia. Only one other element of marketing cost averaged more than $0.40 per pair sold — customer rebates in North America. No celebrities have been used to promote the company's brand to this point, but several well-known sports celebrities are available as of Year 11 and you and your co-managers will have to decide whether to utilize celebrity endorsements in the future. The amounts paid to celebrities will be allocated to each geographic market based on the percentage of total branded pairs sold.

The last portion of the Cost Report shows a breakdown of administrative expenses per pair sold and interest expenses per pair sold. The per pair costs for each of these cost elements are the same across all four market segments because this is a necessary arithmetic outcome of allocating administrative and interest costs to each segment based on each segment's share of pairs sold. As you can see from the last line on the report, total costs per pair sold vary significantly from segment to segment — thus explaining the need for different prices in different market segments.

THE INCOME STATEMENT

Table 2-6 presents the Income Statement for Year 10. Revenues for the year totaled $82,810,000, operating profit was $13,390,000, and net income after taxes was $7,481,000. North American footwear sales contributed 79% of total operating profits ($10,555,000 out of $13,390,000).

Table 2-6: INCOME STATEMENT, YEAR 10

	– North America –				
	P-Label	**Branded**	**Europe**	**Asia**	**Overall**
Sales Revenues	$14,170	$42,500	$17,500	$8,640	$82,810
Manufact. Cost of Goods Sold	9,616	27,091	9,225	4,501	50,433
Warehouse Expenses	1,046	2,655	3,576	3,130	10,407
Marketing Expenses	0	3,950	1,465	666	6,081
Administrative Expenses	502	1,255	502	241	2,500
Operating Profit (Loss)	3,005	7,550	2,733	102	13,390
Extraordinary Gain (Loss)					0
Interest Income (Expense)					(2,702)
Income Before Taxes					10,687
Income Taxes					3,206
Net Income					$7,481
Earnings Per Share					$1.50

Gains or losses on plant sales and permanent plant closings are accounted for as an extraordinary item and affect before-tax income. If you and your co-managers negotiate the sale of all or part of a plant at a price ***above*** the prevailing book value of that capacity (as measured by the value of the capacity after depreciation), then your company realizes a taxable extraordinary gain on the transaction equal to the difference between selling price and book value. The net investment in each plant appears on each year's Manufacturing Report. If you and your co-managers sell plant capacity at a price ***below*** net book value, then your company realizes a loss equal to the amount that the selling price is below the remaining net investment on the books. When a plant is permanently closed, the liquidation value is 25% of net investment insofar as the Ohio plant is concerned and 75% of net investment for all other plants. The losses associated with a plant shutdown appear on the Income Statement as an extraordinary loss.

Interest expenses on short-term loans and long-term bonds are deducted from operating profit to arrive at before-tax income. Interest expenses are shown as a companywide expense on the Income Statement. ***The company pays an income tax rate of 30%.*** Taxes owed are calculated as a straight 30% of income before taxes. After-tax losses may be carried over for ***three*** years in determining your company's tax liability. Thus, if your company should have an after-tax loss of $500,000 in one year, your company will have a $500,000 tax-loss carry-forward to deduct against before-tax income the following three years until the $500,000 "tax credit" is used up.

THE BALANCE SHEET

Table 2-7 presents your company's Balance Sheet at the end of Year 10. Total assets amounted to $69,242,000, of which $42,785,000 represented investment in the Ohio and Texas plants. The accounts receivable of $20,702,000 represents 25% of Year 10 sales revenues that will be collected in Year 11; retailers do not pay for shoes shipped during the last quarter of the year until after January 1. Current liabilities consist of accounts payable plus short-term loans. The company's one account payable consists of 25% of Year 10 materials purchased from suppliers that do not have to be paid for until January 1 of Year 11; all other expenses incurred in Year 10, including income taxes, are paid no later than the last day of each year and thus do not represent year-end liabilities.

Any short-term loan taken out to help finance company operations shows up as a current liability since the note is due the following year; no short-term loan was taken out in Year 10. Long-term debt amounts to $26,100,000 and is in the form of two bonds with annual payments and fixed interest rates as shown in Note 2. The company has 5,000,000 shares of stock outstanding, as shown in Note 3. Total stockholder's equity going into Year 11 is $37,392,000.

> *The debt-to-assets ratio and times-interest-earned coverage ratio are the two financial measures used to determine your company's bond rating.*

The company's debt-to-assets ratio at the end of Year 10 was .38 ($26,600,000 in ***total*** debt divided by $69,242,000); in calculating this ratio, ***debt is defined as the sum of long-term bonds outstanding and short-term loans.*** A debt-to-asset ratio below .25 (or 25%) is considered by creditors as quite good from a risk standpoint; a ratio greater than .50 (or 50%) is considered high and will adversely affect the company's creditworthiness.

The times-interest-earned ratio is calculated by dividing companywide operating profit by total interest expenses (both are shown on the Income Statement). In Year 10 your company's times-interest-earned ratio was a healthy 4.96 ($13,390,000 ÷ $2,702,000 = 4.96), meaning that the company's operating profits were big enough to cover current interest payment obligations by a factor of almost 5 times. A coverage ratio of 2.0 is considered minimum by risk-conscious bondholders and bond buyers because a sudden drop-off in sales or an unexpected cash expense can crimp a company's cash flows and imperil its ability to meet its interest payment obligations.

Table 2-7: Balance Sheet, Year 10

Assets:		
Cash on Hand	$ 311	
Accounts Receivable	20,702	
Footwear Inventories	5,444	
Total Current Assets		$26,457
Gross Plant Investment	55,300	
Accumulated Depreciation	12,515	
Net Plant Investment		42,785
Total Assets		69,242
Liabilities and Stockholders' Equity:		
Accounts Payable	5,250	
Short-Term Loan Payable (see Note 1)	500	
Total Current Liabilities		5,750
Long-Term Bonds Outstanding (see Note 2)		26,100
Total Liabilities		31,850
Common Stock (see Note 3)		5,000
Additional Stockholders' Capital (see Note 4)		16,000
Accumulated Retained Earnings (see Note 5)		16,392
Total Stockholders' Equity		37,392
Total Liabilities and Stockholders' Equity		$69,242

Note 1: The short-term loan carries an interest rate of 6.50%.

Note 2: Long-term bonds outstanding:

Bond Number	Year Issued	Outstanding Principal	Annual Payment	Interest Rate
1	Year 7	$12,600	$1,800	10.40%
2	Year 9	$13,500	$1,500	8.45%
3				
4				
5				
6				
7				
8				
9				
10				

Note 3: Common stock carries a par value of $1.00 per share. There are 5,000,000 shares issued with a minimum of 3,000,000 and a maximum of 50,000,000 shares outstanding.

Note 4: Additional stockholders' capital is a measure of the amount that shareholders have invested in the company's common stock over and above par value.

Note 5: Accumulated retained earnings is a summation of the after-tax profits the company has earned over all its years of operation that have not been paid out in the form of dividends.

The covenants in the company's bonds outstanding preclude the issue of any new bonds unless the previous year's times-interest-earned coverage ratio was 2.0 or greater. Hence, in order to guarantee your company's access to the bond market in the years to come, you and your co-managers will have to monitor the times-interest-earned coverage closely and do everything you can to keep it above 2.0 each year.

THE CASH FLOW REPORT

The Cash Flow Report provides a convenient summary of annual cash inflows and annual cash disbursements. Total cash available from all sources amounted to $80,174,000 in Year 10, consisting of a $1,397,000 beginning cash balance and collections from footwear sales of $78,277,000 — see Table 2-8. The company grants three months credit to retailers; retailers take advantage of this credit policy and do not pay for shipments received after October 1 until the beginning of the following year. Since footwear sales to retailers occur evenly across the months of the year, collections from footwear sales always amount to 25% of prior-year sales plus 75% of current-year sales; this accounts for why cash inflow from footwear sales does not match exactly with annual revenues reported on the Income Statement.[6]

Table 2-8: CASH FLOW REPORT, YEAR 10

Cash Inflows:	
Beginning Cash Balance	$ 1,397
Receipts from Footwear Sales	78,277
New Bond Issues	0
New Stock Issues	0
Sale or Liquidation of Plant Capacity	0
Short-Term Loan (at an interest rate of 6.50%)	500
Refunds (Fines)	0
Total Cash Inflows	$80,174
Cash Outflows:	
Payments to Materials Suppliers	$19,647
Operations (production, warehouse, marketing, and administrative)	49,008
Payments for New Equipment and/or New Plant Capacity	0
Bond Repayments (includes early bond retirement)	3,300
Bond Interest (includes prepayment penalty)	2,765
Short-Term Loan Repayment	0
Short-Term Interest Expense (Income)	(63)
Stock Repurchases	0
Income Tax Payment	3,206
Dividend Payment	2,000
Total Cash Outflows	$79,864
Net Cash Balance (inflows – outflows)	$311

Cash from bond issues and stock issues is received in the same year such issues are made. Cash from the sale of a plant is received at the beginning of the following year. Cash from any plant liquidation is received in the ***same year*** the decision on permanent plant closing is made — plant shutdowns take effect at the beginning of the year and no production from the plant is available.

[6] *Company accountants, relying upon generally accepted accounting principles, base income statement revenues on total footwear sales during the calendar year. Actual cash collections from footwear sales do not equal* ***annual*** *revenues because of the year-to-year lags in receiving payments for all footwear shipped between October 1 and December 31 of each year.*

Cash outflows are itemized in the second section of Table 2-8; the amounts paid out for operations correspond to the costs appearing in the manufacturing, warehouse and sales, and marketing and administrative reports. The payments for materials, however, consist of 25% of material costs for the previous year plus 75% of material costs for the current year since suppliers are not paid for materials used after October 1 of each year until after January 1. The bond repayments of $3,300,000 went to reduce the principal owed on bonds 1 and 2 (see Note 2 on the Year 10 Balance Sheet). The bond interest of $2,765,000 stemmed from the principal outstanding on bonds 1 and 2. The company had no short-term loan from Year 9 to repay in Year 10. However, the company had net interest income for the year of $63,000 because the company's banks pay interest on the company's beginning-year cash balances equal to the going prime rate less 3%. The company's beginning cash balance in Year 10 was $1,397,000; the interest rate paid by the banks on this balance was 4.5% (the Year 10 prime rate on short-term loans was 7.5%), yielding interest income of $62,865. Income tax obligations of $3,206,000 incurred on Year 10 profits were paid in Year 10; it is company practice to pay all income taxes owed at year-end so as to stay current on income tax liabilities. Dividend payments in Year 10 totaled $2,000,000, equal to $0.40 per share of common stock.

Using The Company Reports

After each year's decisions are "processed," you will receive all eight of these reports detailing how your company fared. The reports provide information essential in assessing the results of the past year and developing next year's strategy and decisions. You need to become very familiar with all of the information in the Year 10 reports since they define your company's situation heading into Year 11.

Section 3

STRATEGIES AND DECISIONS

This section highlights the strategic and operating issues confronting your company and describes the decisions you and your co-managers must make each period. You will find that computer entry of your decisions makes it easy to explore the revenue-cost-profit economics of different decisions and to do all kinds of what-iffing to see which of the various strategy alternatives is most promising. All the number-crunching is done by the computer in seconds. Procedures for scoring your company's performance, doing a 5-year strategic plan, and using the two disks accompanying this manual are explained in Sections 4 and 5.

PERTINENT STRATEGIC ISSUES

The description of the industry environment and your company's situation presented in Sections 1 and 2 should have left no doubt that you and your co-managers have several strategic issues to confront over the next several decision periods:

1. What competitive strategy should the company follow and what kind of competitive advantage should it try to build?
2. How should you position the company's products in the world footwear market so as to capitalize on the excellent growth opportunities which exist? Which market segments should the company concentrate on?
3. Where should new production capacity be located, given the market growth that is projected?

At present, the company has no sharply-defined strategy for competing. It charges an average price for its footwear, has an average quality product, provides an average level of service to retailers, has an average number of models for customers to select from, and has built an average brand name image via its advertising, retailer network, and rebate efforts. In other words, the company's shoes are not presently differentiated from those of rivals. Costs per pair are on a par with other rivals — the company is neither a low-cost producer nor a high-cost producer. The company is viewed as a "middle-of-the-road" competitor that is trying to participate across-the-board in all four segments of the world footwear market. The company has an average market share in each of the four market segments but is not truly a recognized leader with a dominant position in any phase of the industry.

Closely related to the issue of how to become a more effective competitor is the issue of how to position the company's products in the global marketplace. Prior management was unsure whether the company should pursue both the branded and private-label segments and whether it made sense to strive for market leadership in all three geographic regions simultaneously. And in trying to broaden the company's geographic market base, prior management was unsure whether the company should produce essentially the same quality shoes for all market segments or whether to make high quality shoes for one or two markets and low-quality shoes for the others. You and your co-managers will have the latitude to pursue a low-cost/low-price strategy in one market arena and a high quality/premium price/strong brand image strategy in another market arena should you choose to do so.

Then there is the question of where to locate additional production capacity. The Texas plant can be expanded and serve as a production base for exporting footwear to other parts of the world market. Or, plants can be built in Europe or Asia. A European plant is economically attractive because of the potential distribution cost savings (tariff avoidance and lower shipping costs) on future sales made in Europe; plant sites in Spain or Italy also offer more ample labor supplies and lower wage costs than in Texas. An Asian plant is economically attractive partly because of potential distribution cost savings on future sales in Asia but mainly because of very low wage rates. A large-scale Asian plant could become the company's principal production site, with pairs being exported to Europe and North America to meet growing demand in those markets. There are advantages to having plants in all three geographic areas, and there are economy-of-scale advantages to having one or two large plants as opposed to three or four smaller plants. You'll have to decide what sort of plant configuration best fits your strategy.

You and your co-managers have the authority to pursue whatever business strategy you wish and to revise it as needed. *The Business Strategy Game* provides great leeway in crafting strategy, with ***no built-in favoritism*** shown to one strategy over another. Most any prudent business strategy has potential for succeeding, ***provided it is not overpowered by the actions and strategies of rival companies.*** Since market outcomes are determined by how your company's competitive effort stacks up against the efforts of rivals and since it is safe to assume that rival companies will try to outmaneuver and outcompete your company, you and your co-managers will have to watch competitors' actions closely and try to anticipate their moves when developing your company's strategy and making decisions. You will have to stay on top of changing market conditions, try to avoid being outmaneuvered or put into a competitive bind by the actions of rival companies, and make sure your footwear products are attractively-priced and competitively marketed. Whether your company becomes an industry leader will depend on how the caliber of your company's strategies and operating decisions stack up against the caliber of the strategies and decisions of rival companies.

> ***Most any prudent business strategy has potential for succeeding; there is no built-in favoritism shown to one strategy over another.***

PERTINENT OPERATING ISSUES

In the Section 2 presentation of your company's results for Year 10, several operating issues were mentioned that need management attention:

1. What to do about the high manufacturing costs at the Ohio plant.
2. Whether cost-saving efficiencies can be implemented in any portion of the cost chain (use of materials, manufacturing, shipping and warehousing, marketing, and administration).

3. Whether to continue to offer the same number of models/styles and the same quality shoes in all market segments where the company competes.
4. Whether to make base pay and incentive compensation adjustments at the Ohio and Texas plants in Year 11.
5. What to do in Year 11 to get ready to meet the expected (average) demand of 3,750,000 pairs in Year 12.

You can take decisive action to resolve these issues quickly or adopt a cautious "wait-and-see" posture and defer actions until later. As for item 5, you have five options to try to handle the expected 3,750,000-pair demand in Year 12, given the present plant capacity of 3,000,000 pairs:

- Build up inventories in Year 11 by producing at full capacity (or at overtime) and use what is unsold at year-end to help meet retailer demand in Year 12.
- Use heavy overtime in Year 12 to meet Year 12 demand; with maximum overtime, your plants should be able to turn out 3,600,000 pairs (less the pairs rejected for unacceptable quality).
- Focus on a narrow portion of the total market in Year 12, be content with slower growth and below average sales volume for a year, concentrate on profitability in Year 12, and decide on expansion later.
- Launch an expansion of the Texas plant in Year 11 to be ready in Year 12.
- Construct a new plant in Europe or Asia in Year 11 to be ready in Year 12.

The first three options are more conservative in the sense that they give you more time to assess the market and decide upon a long-range production and capacity expansion strategy. The last two options entail making a strategic commitment that you must be prepared to live with in the future.

Prevailing Costs and Rates

After you have thoroughly studied the results for Year 10 (as presented in the eight reports shown in Section 2) and are familiar with company operations, you are ready to begin the task of making a decision for Year 11 and thinking about a long-term strategy. Listed in Table 3-1 is a summary of key costs and rates that prevailed industrywide in Year 10. This listing is important for two reasons: one, it indicates key values that you need to be familiar with and, two, it indicates the specific items which are subject to change (up or down) as the game progresses.

Table 3-1: Prevailing Costs and Rates

Interest Rates	**AAA Bonds**	7.50%
	Short-Term Prime	7.50%
Base Materials Prices ($ per pair)	**Normal-Wear**	6.00
	Long-Wear	12.00
Base Plant Supervision Cost ($ per worker)		5,000
Private-Label Specs	**Minimum Models**	50
	Minimum Quality	50
Private-Label Conversion Cost ($ per pair)		0.25
Shipping Costs ($ per pair)	**Within a Region**	0.25
	Between Regions	0.50

Import Tariffs ($ per pair)	**N.A. to Europe**	4.00
	N.A. to Asia	8.00
	Europe to N.A.	0.00
	Europe to Asia	8.00
	Asia to N.A.	0.00
	Asia to Europe	4.00
Cost of Faster Delivery	**3-weeks**	0.25
	2-weeks	0.75
	1-week	1.50
Retailer Support Cost ($/retail outlet)		100
Cost of Bid for Celebrities ($000s)		100

The figures in Table 3-1 will prevail for Year 11 unless otherwise indicated by the instructor or game administrator. The instructor/game administrator will inform you as the game progresses of the latest exchange rates, interest rates, and S&P 500 Index value. Unless the instructor/game administrator tells you otherwise, expect pertinent Year 11 values to be announced prior to the Year 11 decision, pertinent Year 12 values to be announced prior to the Year 12 decision, and so on. Also, expect the upcoming year's interest rates and exchange rates to already be on the company disk and programmed into all calculations the computer provides. If you want to track the S&P 500 Index and the exchange rates for the Eurodollar and Japanese yen, consult page C-1 of each issue of *The Wall Street Journal.*

THE S&P 500 INDEX. Keep in mind that year-to-year increases in the S&P 500 Index will boost footwear sales potentials worldwide whereas year-to-year declines will shrink worldwide market potential. ***The maximum impact is ±10%.*** The S&P 500 Index will have no impact on the Year 11 forecast, however. The S&P 500 Index value for Year 11 is the starting value; ***the first impact of changes in the S&P 500 on forecasted sales potential comes in Year 12.***

> ***There will be no S&P 500 or exchange rate impacts in Year 11. Changes in these rates will first come into play in Year 12.***

EXCHANGE RATES. Do not be concerned if the current exchange rates for Eurodollars and Japanese yen differ greatly from those for Year 10 (as discussed in Section 2 on page 28). All future exchange rate impacts in the game will be based on actual exchange rate fluctuations in the days and weeks ahead (your instructor will inform you of the starting exchange rate values for Year 11). The Year 10 exchange rates will thus have no bearing on your company's operating results in Year 11 and beyond. The change in the exchange rates from Year 11 to Year 12 will determine exchange rate gains or losses for Year 12; the changes from Year 12 to Year 13 will determine the gains or losses in Year 13; and so on. Because the exchange rates announced by your instructor for Year 11 will serve as the base rates for the game, ***there will be no exchange rate change impacts on the Year 11 results; the first round of exchange rate gains and losses will come in Year 12.***

MAKING DECISIONS

When you arrive at the opening screen on the PC, you will be led through a few introductory screens involving entry of an industry number, company letter and name, password, and names and IDs of the management team; then the Main Menu will come up. To begin the decision process, you'll select the Decision Entries option that takes you to all of the decision screens. In the remainder of this section, we will review the decision screens, discuss the decision entries, and explain various relationships, procedures, and "rules" you need to be aware of. When you start work on your decisions, be aggressive in experimenting with a variety of different decision entries and decision combinations. The more that you and your co-managers try out different decisions and observe the different projected outcomes that appear on the screen, the quicker you will come to understand the interconnections among the various decisions and arrive at an acceptable combination of decision entries. ***No entry is final until you give your Company Data Disk to the instructor/game administrator.***

MANUFACTURING DECISIONS

Each decision period you and your co-managers must make a series of decisions concerning plant operations and footwear production. All the decisions made each year are shown on the upper portion of the manufacturing decisions screen (the light-shaded area in Exhibit 3-1). The numbers appearing in the entry columns represent prior management's decisions for Year 10. The boxed entries in the dark-shaded area of the screen represent "what ifs" or "educated guestimates" you and your co-managers will need to make regarding Year 11 outcomes (the numbers in these boxes in Exhibit 3-1 represent actual Year 10 outcomes). The information appearing in the lower portion of the screen represents calculations instantaneously provided by the computer each time you make a decision entry or a what if entry (the numbers in the lower portion of the screen in Exhibit 3-1 represent Year 10 outcomes).

Exhibit 3-1: MANUFACTURING DECISIONS SCREEN

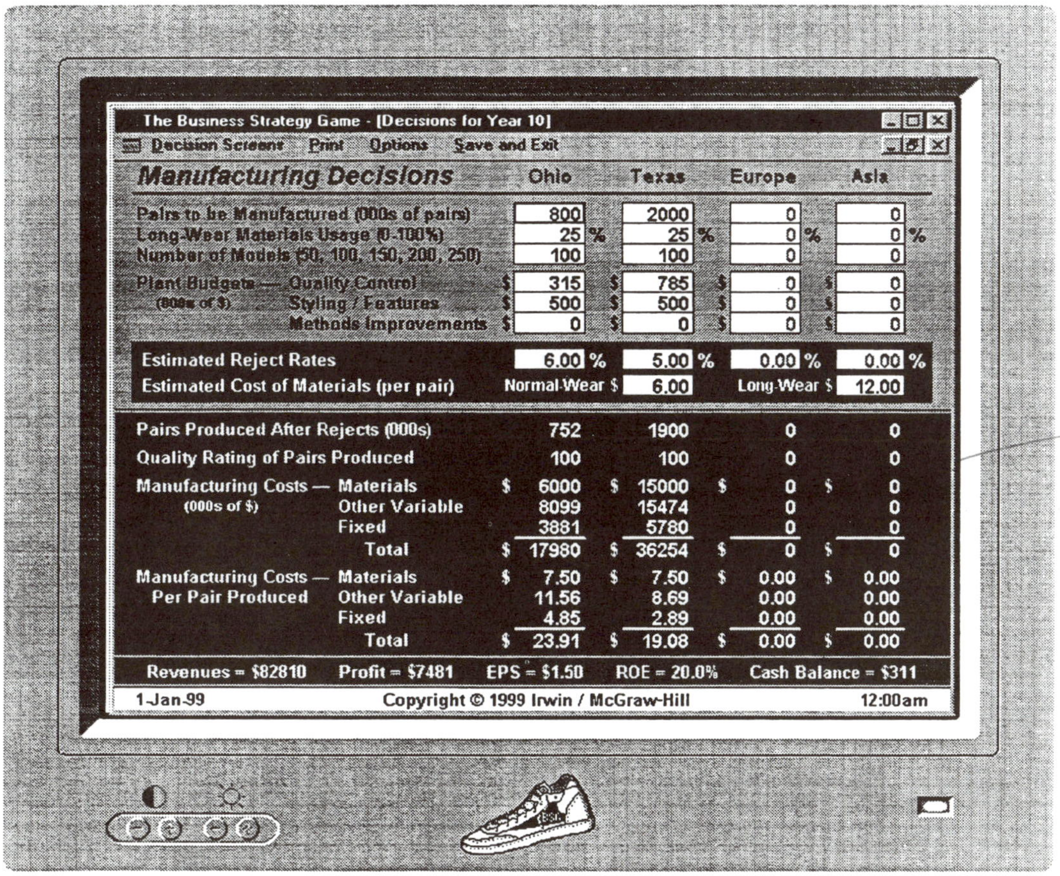

HOW MANY PAIRS TO PRODUCE. The three biggest factors to consider in deciding how many pairs to produce are (1) the number of pairs in inventory in each distribution center that went unsold in Year 10, (2) how many pairs you want to sell in Year 11, and (3) how many pairs you want left in inventory at the end of Year 11 as a safety buffer against stockouts or as a deliberate inventory build-up to support sales in future years. The footwear demand forecasts for Years 11 and 12 are as follows:

	Private-Label Sales Forecast (in pairs)	Branded Sales Forecast (in pairs)			Worldwide Potential (in pairs)
		North America	Europe	Asia	
Year 11	600,000	1,450,000	600,000	350,000	3,000,000
Year 12	700,000	1,820,000	780,000	450,000	3,750,000

These are ***averages per company***. Your company's sales in an area can be more or less than the average, according to whether your company's competitive effort is stronger or weaker than the efforts expended by rival companies. With maximum use of overtime, you can currently produce as many as 1,200,000 pairs at the Ohio plant and as many as 2,400,000 pairs at the Texas plant.

MATERIALS DECISIONS. The only materials-related decision you make concerns the percentage mix of long-wear and normal-wear materials to be used at each plant; "the computer" will automatically take care of ordering the needed amount of materials based on the number of pairs you and your co-managers decide to produce. You and your co-managers may use either the ***same*** normal-wear/long-wear mix at each plant (as in Year 10) or you can use ***different*** percentage mixes. Having the flexibility to vary the mix of normal-wear and long-wear materials from plant to plant allows the company to produce shoes more cheaply at some plants than others by using a lower cost combination of normal-wear and long-wear materials. Producing different quality shoes at different plants can be beneficial if you elect to sell in the private-label footwear segment (where only a quality rating of 50 is needed) or wish to position your company's branded footwear differently on the quality spectrum in different geographic markets.

Keep in mind that the long-wear materials percentage is one of the factors used by the International Footwear Federation in calculating the quality of each plant's output. Assuming no change in the other quality-determining factors, an increase in the long-wear materials percentage will boost the quality of a plant's output and a decrease will lower it. The International Footwear Federation's product quality formula is programmed in so that you can immediately see the impact on product quality of a change in the percentage use of long-wear materials — quality rating projections appear on the second line in the bottom section of Exhibit 3-1. Also, you will be able to see the cost impact of raising/lowering the long-wear materials mix by watching the changes in manufacturing cost per pair produced (in the lower portion of the screen) as you make different entries for the long-wear percentage.

DECISIONS REGARDING THE NUMBER OF MODELS. You and your co-managers have the option at each plant of producing 50, 100, 150, 200, or 250 models. Production run set-up costs are currently $1,000,000 per plant for making 50 models and increase $1,000,000 for each 50-model increment (up to $5,000,000 for 250 models). How many models you and your co-managers elect to produce at each plant will have a sizable impact on *per pair* production costs. At the Ohio plant, for example, producing 1,000,000 pairs and 50 models entails production run set-up costs of $1.00 per pair whereas producing 1,000,000 pairs and 250 models entails set-up costs of $5.00 per pair. At the bigger Texas plant, however, producing 2,000,000 pairs and 250 models results in set-up costs of just $2.50 per pair. The number of models produced at each plant also affects the number of defective pairs. ***The more models produced, the higher the reject rate***; this is because more frequent production run change-overs result in reduced worker experience and skill in making each model.

> ***The wider the selection of models/styles offered, the wider the appeal of your product line, but unless corrective measures are taken, more models will increase reject rates and decrease quality ratings.***

It is important to understand that producing 100 models in Ohio and 100 models in Texas entails producing the ***same*** set of 100 models at each plant, ***not*** entirely different sets of models/styles. When footwear from different plants producing different numbers of models/styles is shipped to a particular distribution warehouse (Memphis, Brussels, or Singapore), the resulting number of models/styles available to buyers in the market served by that warehouse equals the weighted average number of models. For example, if the Ohio plant produces 1,000,000 pairs and 50 models and the Texas plant produces 2,000,000 pairs and 100 models and if 400,000 pairs from each plant are then shipped to the Brussels warehouse, model availability in Europe will be an average of 75 models/styles (assuming no inventory of pairs in Brussels). If there are already some pairs in inventory in Brussels, the 75 figure will be adjusted up or down based on the models in inventory.

The number of models your company makes available in each geographic market is ***a big driver*** of your company's branded sales and market share. The wider the selection of models/styles offered (shoes for men, women, and children, and styles suitable for running, jogging, aerobics, basketball, tennis, golf, casual wear, etc.), the wider the appeal of your product line. ***Other things being equal (price, quality, brand image, service, and so on), companies with a bigger selection of models in a particular geographic region will outsell companies with a smaller selection.***

DECISIONS REGARDING QUALITY CONTROL AND STYLING/FEATURES. How much you and your co-managers decide to spend for quality control and styling/features at each plant affects the International Footwear Federation's ratings of product quality at each plant. Remember that the Federation's quality ratings are based on (1) the company's overall long-term quality control effort (as measured by the company's ***cumulative*** quality control expenditure ***per pair produced*** at all plants for all years), (2) ***current-year*** expenditures for quality control ***per pair produced*** (which reflects plant efforts to reinforce the quality control effort of prior years and, if expenditures are sizable enough, to further enhance the quality of the plant's output), (3) styling/features expenditures ***per model/style produced*** at each plant, and (4) the percentage of long-wear materials used at each plant. As you make entries for models, quality control, and styling/features on the manufacturing screen, the computer is programmed with the International Footwear Federation's formula to immediately calculate product quality at each plant — see the entries on line 2 in the bottom section of the manufacturing decisions screen. You can enter different values for models, quality control, and styling/features until you are satisfied with the resulting quality and the production cost per pair. Because the quality of footwear produced at one plant is affected by the company's overall cumulative quality control effort, it is possible for changes in spending (up or down) at one plant to spill over to affect the quality of footwear output at another plant.

> ***The four factors that determine PRODUCT QUALITY are:***
> - ***Long-wear materials percentage***
> - ***Quality control expenditures per pair produced (in current year)***
> - ***Cumulative quality control expenditures per pair produced***
> - ***Styling/features budget per model***

DECISIONS REGARDING PRODUCTION METHODS IMPROVEMENT. This decision option allows you to budget dollars for continuous improvements in work practices and plant efficiency. ***The money you spend at a particular plant for methods improvements acts to (1) reduce materials costs at the plant by as much as 25%, (2) reduce supervision costs in the plant by as much as 25%, and (3) increase the annual productivity of the workers in that plant by as much as 500 pairs per worker per year.***

> ***Expenditures for PRODUCTION METHODS IMPROVEMENTS in a particular plant act to:***
> - ***Reduce materials costs***
> - ***Reduce plant supervision costs***
> - ***Increase worker productivity***

The cost reduction and productivity-increasing benefits your company will realize from expenditures on production methods improvement are a function of the ***average annual amount spent per pair of production capacity***. Because the benefits depend on the *average annual* amount spent per pair of production capacity, you should view such expenditures as part of an ongoing effort to drive costs down rather than as something to be done intermittently — for example, if you spend $1.00 per pair on production methods improvement in Year 11 and $0 per pair in Year 12, the annual average drops to $0.50 in Year 12. Likewise, a plant expansion will reduce the average amount spent per pair unless total spending for methods improvements is increased in proportion to production capacity. Also, there are diminishing marginal benefits to spending additional sums for production methods improvement — the incremental benefits from increasing spending from $0.20 per pair to $0.40 per pair of capacity will exceed the benefits associated with increasing spending from $0.40 to $0.60 per pair; and so on. Studies indicate that you will probably have to maintain average spending levels in the neighborhood of $1.00 per pair of production capacity to achieve 50 - 60% of the benefits and $2 per pair or more to realize the full benefits of production methods improvements.

Expenditures for improved production methods have the same impact in all plants; that is, spending an average of $0.05 per pair of capacity will have the same impact in reducing materials costs in a Texas or Ohio plant as a European or Asian plant. However, ***methods improvement expenditures will have a bigger impact on reducing plant supervision costs and boosting worker productivity in your company's Ohio and Texas plants than for new plants that might be constructed in Europe or Asia***; this is because the Ohio and Texas plants are older and involve less efficient plant layouts and work methods than plants constructed after Year 10. The overall biggest "bang for the buck" from spending on methods improvements occurs in the Ohio plant because of that plant's less efficient shoe-making practices and production layout.

> ***Production methods improvement expenditures will have a bigger impact in the Ohio and Texas plants than in newer European or Asian plants.***

WHAT-IF ESTIMATES. There are two production-related uncertainties which come into play in each year's manufacturing decisions:

1. ***The costs your company will incur for raw materials*** — The market prices for materials will vary above or below the "regular" or base prices (currently $6.00 per pair for normal-wear materials and $12.00 for long-wear materials) whenever industrywide capacity utilization rates fall outside the 90% to 100% range and/or whenever the long-wear percentage deviates from the 25% industrywide benchmark. You will find year-to-year variations in the market prices for materials to be a common occurrence. (See the discussion of raw materials supplies in Section 1 for more details.) Furthermore, your company's cost for materials can actually be lower than the going market prices for materials because of the materials cost savings associated with cumulative per pair expenditures for production methods improvements.
2. ***The reject rate on total pairs produced*** — Reject rates are a function of the piece rate incentive, annual quality control expenditures, and number of models produced. Unless notified otherwise by your instructor/game administrator, the standard reject rate is 6% for the Ohio plant and 5% for all other plants. Higher piecework incentives pull reject rates down because of increased worker attention to accurate craftsmanship. Higher annual quality control expenditures per pair produced also translate into lower reject rates, reflecting the benefits of training workers in total quality management techniques. Reject rates automatically fall as fewer models are produced because of greater worker expertise in making each model and less frequent production run change-overs. All defective pairs are donated to charity and represent dead-weight cost and lost revenues.

To take these uncertainties into account and see how your company's manufacturing costs are affected, you and your co-managers can develop "educated guesses" about what your company's materials costs per pair and reject rates might be in the upcoming year. Think of these guestimates as "what-if projections." By entering different what-if values for these two variables in the dark-shaded box on the manufacturing decisions screen, you can ascertain the upside and downside impact of different materials costs and reject rates. Trying both optimistic and pessimistic what-if values will show you how sensitive manufacturing costs, revenues, profits, earnings per share, and ROE are to different material costs and reject rate outcomes. If you are unwilling to venture a judgment about what might happen to materials costs and reject rates in the upcoming year, you can simply go with the values for last year. The computer uses whatever what-if values are entered in these cells in calculating all the revenue-cost-profit

Number of worker to avoid over time
Stock out controlled by shipping 1 week 3 week
Number of workers employed must be able to produce required products
short delivery
Annual wages
% of total package is incentive base ⇒ Determines productivity
Incentive Pay

projections for the upcoming year, so the more accurate your what-if projections the more accurate the calculations of the upcoming year's performance will be. Astute what-iffing on your part will improve the accuracy of company performance projections and help avert performance surprises.

LABOR DECISIONS

The labor decisions made by prior management in Year 10 are shown on the labor decisions screen (Exhibit 3-2).

Exhibit 3-2: LABOR DECISIONS SCREEN

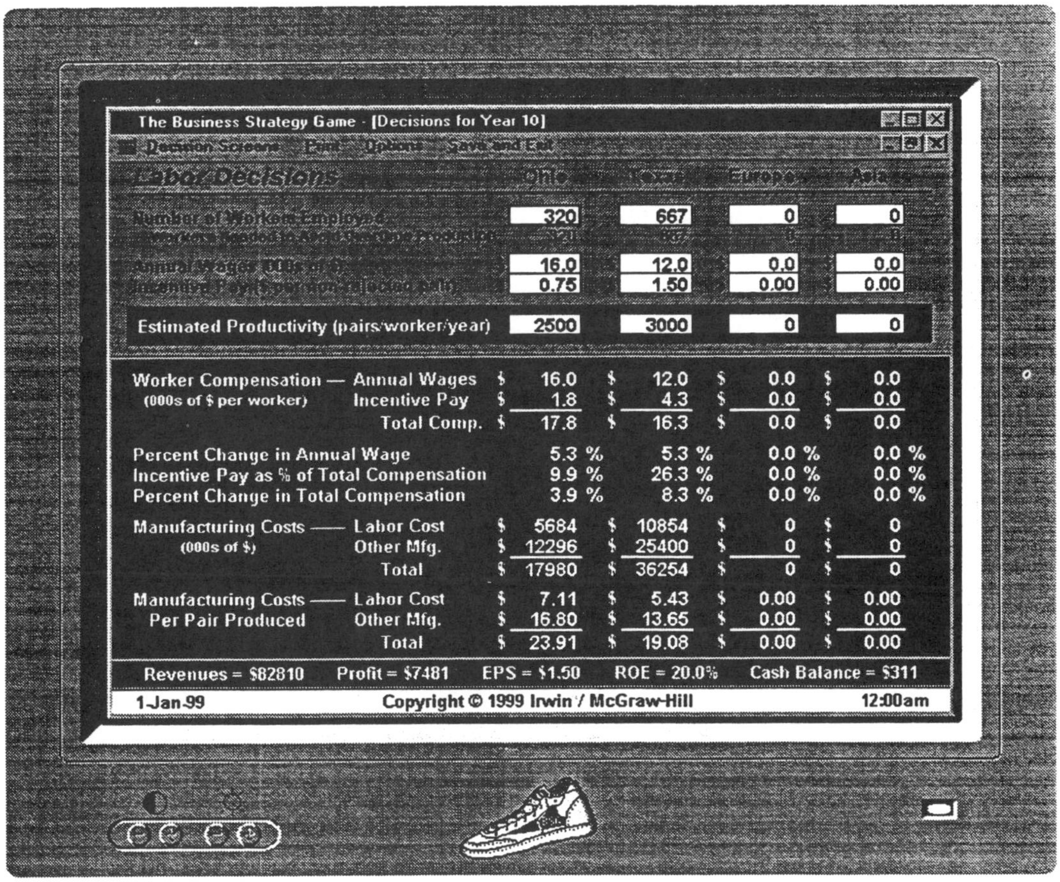

How many workers you will need to hire is a function of how many pairs you intend to produce and your estimate of what worker productivity will turn out to be. For instance, if the decision is to produce 2,000,000 pairs in Texas and if estimated worker productivity is 3,000 pairs per year (as it was in Year 10), then you will need to employ 667 workers (2,000,000 pairs ÷ 3,000 = 667). The computer will automatically calculate the number of workers needed based on (1) the worker productivity value that appears in the what-if cell (this will almost always be last year's worker productivity value for the plant unless you change it to make your own "what-if projection" for the upcoming year) and (2) the pairs to be manufactured (the first entry on the manufacturing decisions screen) — the calculation of workers needed is based on avoiding the use of overtime. You and your co-managers may elect to employ fewer workers than shown (and produce some shoes at overtime) or employ several more than needed (as a hedge against overestimating worker productivity). Hiring fewer workers than needed and relying on some use of overtime acts to reduce plant supervision costs — currently, plant supervision costs are $5,000 per worker employed. It is a simple what-iffing exercise to try hiring less workers than needed to see if overtime production is economical — don't be surprised if the answer varies by plant because of the differences in worker compensation.

In deciding upon the annual wage, you can grant a wage increase, leave the wage as is, or institute a wage cut. ***You can expect a wage cut, even a small one, to hurt worker productivity.*** The larger the cut the bigger the adverse impact because wage cuts will boost work force turnover (some of the company's best workers will leave for better paying jobs elsewhere), reduce the morale and job satisfaction of the remaining work force, and result in the hiring of less experienced (less productive) workers. Base wages are entered in thousands, but you can establish a wage out to the nearest hundred dollars — like $12,400 or $16,900, but ***not*** $12,450 or $16,925. A wage of $12,400 is entered as 12.4; a wage of $16,900 is entered as 16.9.

> ***You can expect a base wage cut, even a small one, to hurt worker productivity.***

> ***The minimum annual wage for Texas and Ohio plants is $10,000; in Europe the minimum is $9,000 and in Asia it is $2,500.***

Increases in the annual wage will boost labor productivity. Base wage increases in the 5-10% range can lead to productivity gains of as much as 6%. However, as the size of the annual wage increase approaches 12% in any one year, the productivity gains flatten out. Past 12%, the only productivity benefit you can gain comes from a more favorable comparison with the compensation packages of rival companies.

Paying workers a piecework incentive helps reduce reject rates and produces a ***continuing*** boost to productivity year after year — a $1.50 per pair bonus incentive offered in Year 11 will motivate workers to produce more pairs in Year 11 and it will motivate them to achieve still higher productivity levels in Year 12, Year 13, and afterward even if the $1.50 incentive is not increased. The bigger the piecework incentive per pair, the bigger the reduction in reject rates. The larger the percentage of workers' total compensation coming from piecework bonuses, the larger the ***annual*** boost to worker productivity. However, ***once incentive pay exceeds 25% of total compensation, the incremental gains in productivity become progressively smaller; past 50% of total compensation, there are no gains in productivity attributable to higher incentive compensation*** — but you can still derive some productivity gains from more favorable comparisons with the compensation packages of rival companies. Companies with the highest compensation packages (wages plus total incentive pay) will attract workers with good experience, good skills, and good work habits and will, ***other things being equal***, have higher levels of worker productivity than companies on the low end of the pay scale.

Consequently, you and your co-managers will need to consider carefully the size of annual wage increases, the size of piecework incentives, the percent of total compensation accounted for by incentive pay, and how well your workers are being compensated relative to workers at competing companies (pay comparisons are reported annually in the Footwear Industry Report). We urge you to monitor the size of resulting productivity gains and determine whether your compensation practices are really cost-effective (consult the Benchmarking Report that provides labor cost comparisons to see if your company is overpaying for the productivity gains realized).

MAKING WHAT-IF ESTIMATES OF WORKER PRODUCTIVITY. If you believe that the wage and piecework incentives you decide upon (along with any expenditures for methods improvements) will boost productivity, then you should make new what-if productivity guestimates for each plant, check the computer's recalculation of the workers needed, and adjust the number of workers employed accordingly.

> ***Higher productivity does NOT increase plant capacity; it improves labor efficiency.***

Since your what-if worker productivity value is likely to be "off" by some amount, you and your co-managers will have to decide whether to risk hiring more workers than might actually be needed or use overtime to make up for any shortfall. The use of overtime to cover the uncertainty over labor productivity is fairly simple to handle. For example, if you want to produce 2,000,000 pairs in Texas and are unsure whether labor productivity will reach 3,100 pairs, you can still go ahead and hire only 645 workers (2,000,000 pairs ÷ 3,100 pairs per workers = 645 workers needed). If productivity turns out to be only 3,050 pairs in Texas, resulting in regular-time production of 1,967,250 pairs (found by multiplying 3,050 pairs times 645 workers), the balance of 32,750 pairs will automatically be produced at overtime by the 645 workers. Whether it is cheaper to use overtime in this manner or, instead, to use a conservative worker productivity estimate (say 3,025 pairs per worker) and hire as many 661 workers to produce the 2,000,000 pairs is left for you to analyze using the calculations provided at the bottom of the labor decisions screen. In watching all the on-screen cost calculations following each decision or what-if entry, keep in mind that each reduction in worker head-count reduces total plant supervision costs (currently, by $5,000 per worker).

SHIPPING DECISIONS

The Warehouse and Sales Report for Year 10 (see Table 2-2 on page 25) shows the sales and inventories at the company's warehouses at the end of Year 10. Going into Year 11, you have no pairs of private-label shoes in inventory, 155,000 pairs of branded shoes in inventory in North America, 52,000 branded pairs in Europe, and 60,000 branded pairs in Asia.

Unless there are sufficient numbers of pairs in each warehouse to satisfy retailer orders coming from that geographic area (refer back to the bottom of page 45 for estimates of footwear demand by geographic region in upcoming years), your company will experience stockouts. Stockouts have three adverse consequences: (1) your company loses sales that it could otherwise have gotten, (2) retailers whose orders are unfilled will immediately try to obtain the wanted number of pairs from competitors with inventories available (i.e., rival companies will pick up the sales you lost), and (3) your company's service rating will be penalized. Hence it behooves you and your co-managers to produce and ship enough pairs to each distribution warehouse to avoid stockouts.

The shipping decisions you and your co-managers have to make yearly are shown on the shipping decisions screen — Exhibit 3-3. All pairs awaiting shipment should be shipped to one or more of the distribution centers. Pairs intended for sale in the private-label segment must be shipped to the private-label section of the Memphis warehouse; all pairs intended for sale in the North American branded market should be shipped to the branded section of the Memphis warehouse. Branded pairs in the Memphis warehouse ***cannot*** be sold as private-label footwear; however, unsold private-label inventory ***can*** be converted to branded shoes (at a cost which is currently $0.25 per pair) and sold in the North American branded market if you authorize such conversion (this decision option appears on the upcoming private-label marketing decision screen). The quality rating and model availability attached to all private-label pairs converted to branded shoes will be factored into the weighted average quality rating and model availability of the branded pairs available for sale in North America.

> ***Once finished goods have been shipped to a warehouse, they must be sold from that warehouse; footwear cannot be re-shipped in a later year from one warehouse to another.***

As you enter the pairs to be shipped from the company's plants to the company's distribution warehouses, the calculations section on the shipping decision screen (the dark-shaded section on Exhibit 3-3) will immediately provide you with the weighted average quality ratings and model availabilities of all pairs (including leftover inventories) available for sale in

production to distribution
Must ship ⇒ cost money

Beware of stockouts
Demand is too high

the warehouse serving each customer/market segment. This allows you to adjust shipments until you end up with the desired quality ratings and model availabilities in each warehouse. All footwear inventories left unsold in warehouses at the end of a year are carried over (along with the associated number of models and the adjusted quality ratings) to the next year, to be averaged in with the new pairs produced and shipped to the warehouse. Remember that inventory storage costs rise as unsold inventory rises — per pair inventory storage costs ***at each warehouse*** are $0.25 per pair on the first 500,000 pairs, $0.50 per pair for the next 250,000 pairs, $0.75 per pair on all pairs between 750,000 and 1,000,000 pairs, $1.00 per pair on all pairs between 1,000,000 and 1,250,000 pairs, and $1.50 on each unsold pair in excess of 1,250,000 pairs. The 5-point penalty on the quality rating for unsold private-label pairs and the 10-point penalty on unsold branded pairs in beginning inventory is factored into the quality ratings reported on the shipping decisions screen.

Exhibit 3-3: Shipping Decisions Screen

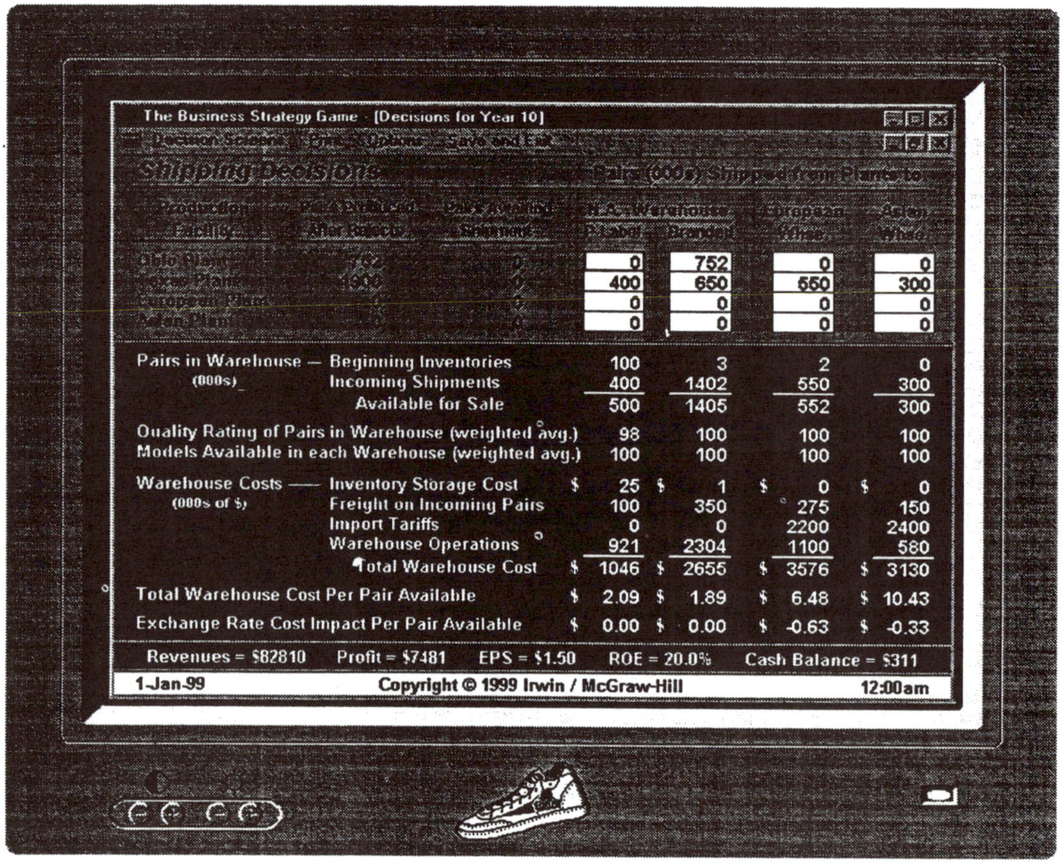

Keep in mind that some uncertainty surrounds how many ***non-defective pairs*** will be produced at your plants and thus be available for shipment. The ***standard reject rates*** are 6.0% for the Ohio plant and 5.0% for all other plants. Last year's reject rates will always appear in the what-if box on the manufacturing decisions screen unless you enter different values. Reject rates at your plants are a function of the number of models produced, annual quality control expenditures per pair produced, and the piecework incentive. If you believe that the decisions you and your co-managers are making ought to cause the reject rates to fall below last year's percentages, enter your what-if "guestimates" for plant reject rates in the appropriate cells on the manufacturing decisions screen. The computer's calculation of the number of pairs awaiting shipment on the shipping decision screen is based on the number of pairs to be produced and on the estimated reject rate (as entered on the manufacturing decisions screen). If the actual number of non-defective pairs produced turns out to be different from the expected number of non-defective pairs (because your what-if projections for worker productivity and/or reject rates were off), then the quantities shipped to each warehouse will automatically be increased or decreased ***proportionally*** to bring total shipments into equality with total pairs available for shipment. In other words, any misestimate of the non-defective pairs available for shipment attributable to inaccurate forecasts of reject rates or worker productivity will be "corrected" during the processing of your decisions.

There is a wealth of other information in the calculations section of the shipping decisions screen to guide your choices of how much to ship where so as to optimize the resulting quality, number of models, inventory levels, costs, and projected profitability.

PLANT DECISIONS

AUTOMATION OPTIONS. You may have robotics-style technology and equipment installed at any of the company's plants. As shown in Table 3-2 below, there are four automation options available for the Ohio and Texas plants and three automation add-ons available for European and Asian plants.

Table 3-2: AUTOMATION OPTIONS

	Availability	Benefits	Capital Cost
Option A	All plants	Increases labor productivity by 500 pairs per worker	$3 million in Ohio plant $5 million in all other plants
Option B	All plants	Reduces production run set-up costs by 40%	$2 million in Ohio plant $4 million in all other plants
Option C	All plants	Reduces plant supervision costs per worker by 25% and reduces production run set-up costs by 25%	$3 million in Ohio plant $5 million in all other plants
Option D	Ohio Plant	Increases labor productivity by 2,000 pairs per worker	$5 million
	Texas Plant	Increases labor productivity by 1,000 pairs per worker	$10 million

You will have to analyze the economics of Options A, B, and C carefully ***because only one of these three options can be used at a given plant during the course of the game*** (because the changes which have to be made in the production line to accommodate the options are not compatible). ***However, at the Ohio and Texas plants you can elect to undertake Option D PLUS one of Options A, B, or C — but only one option can be done in any one year in Texas or Ohio.*** Take time to assess the merits of each automation option because the cost-saving benefits vary quite significantly from plant to plant and strategy to strategy (especially where the number of models is concerned).

Automation options are treated as additional investments, have a 20-year service life depreciated on a straight-line basis at the rate of 5% annually. ***Automation options come on line the year after being ordered.*** Payments to the suppliers of automation options are made the year the option comes on line (i.e. the year after it is ordered). ***An automation option can be ordered for a new plant the first year the new plant is on line***

> ***Automation options are paid for in cash and come on line the year after being ordered.***

or any year thereafter, but you cannot order automation options for a new plant at the same time that the new plant is ordered. The automation options, together with expenditures for production methods improvement, provide your company with alternatives for improving plant efficiency and reducing manufacturing costs per pair produced.

PERMANENTLY CLOSING ALL OR PART OF A PLANT. In the event you decide it is no longer economical to operate a plant or if you have surplus capacity which you are unable to sell to another company, you have the option to permanently close all or part of a plant (in multiples of 1,000,000 pairs). However, newly obtained capacity must be held on the books for at least one year before it is eligible for ***permanent*** closing. ***The cash liquidation value of the Ohio plant is 25% of the company's net investment in the facility; the cash liquidation value of any plant other than Ohio is 75% of the net book value.*** The net investment still on the books for each plant is shown on the company's Manufacturing Report. If you wish to permanently close only part of a plant, the investment write-off is prorated by the percentage of plant capacity closed. For example, if you elect to permanently close one-fourth of a 4,000,000 pair plant having a book value of $40,000,000, then the investment write-off will be $10,000,000, the cash liquidation value of the equipment will be $7,500,000, and the extraordinary loss (written off against current earnings) will be $2,500,000

Exhibit 3-4: PLANT DECISIONS SCREEN

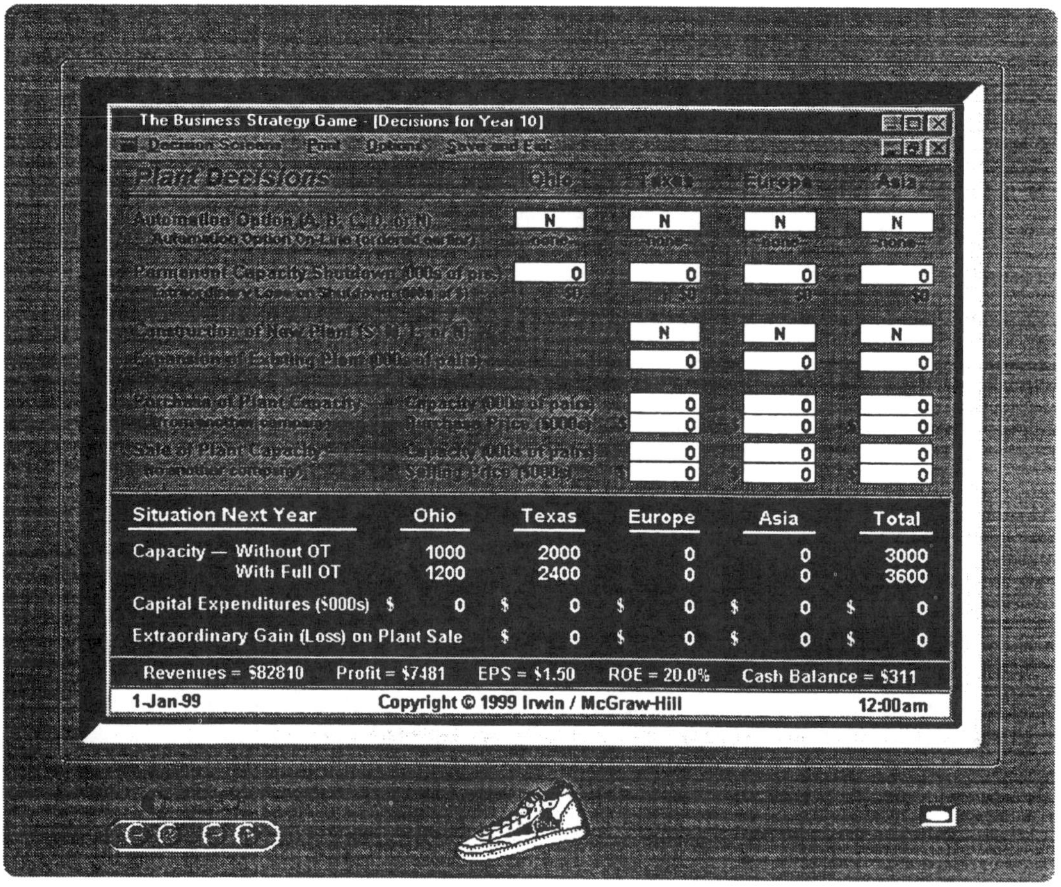

To permanently close a plant, simply indicate how much capacity you wish to shut and at which plant location. Capacity entries are in thousands (enter 1000 to close 1,000,000 pairs of capacity). ***Shutdowns become effective immediately*** (in the same year that the decision is entered), the loss incurred will be charged against current year earnings (appearing as an extraordinary loss on the income statement), and the cash from the liquidation sale will be received and available immediately. Since ***the shutdown occurs at the beginning of the year in which the shutdown decision is made***, the plant capacity in question may not be used for production that year.

Permanent capacity shutdowns take effect at the beginning of the year in which the shutdown decision is entered.

PLANT CONSTRUCTION AND PLANT EXPANSION ALTERNATIVES. Since the Texas plant was built, bigger plant sizes have become technologically feasible and construction costs have changed. Three plant sizes are now available: small (1,000,000 pairs per year), medium (2,000,000 pairs per year), and large (3,000,000 pairs per year). To construct a new plant in Europe or Asia, simply enter S, M, or L; ***it will come on line at the beginning of the following year***. All plants in Texas, Europe, and Asia, regardless of size, can be expanded in increments of 1 million pairs; ***expansions are ready for full production the year after being ordered***. There is no limit on the number of times a plant can be expanded; however, the size of any one expansion is limited to 9,000,000 pairs. Because the Texas plant and any new plants built in Europe and Asia can be expanded to any size, thereby providing whatever amount of production capacity you desire in any geographic region, the company is limited to a maximum of four plants — one in Ohio, one in Texas, one in Europe, and one in Asia. ***The Ohio plant cannot be expanded due to space limitations at the converted warehouse site.***

Table 3-3: THE COST OF NEW PLANTS AND PLANT EXPANSIONS

	Cost of New Plant Construction			Cost of Plant
	Small (1,000,000 pairs)	Medium (2,000,000 pairs)	Large (3,000,000 pairs)	Expansions (per 1,000,000 pairs)
Year 11	$25,000,000	$48,000,000	$70,000,000	$24,000,000
Year 12	25,900,000	49,700,000	72,500,000	24,800,000
Year 13	26,800,000	51,400,000	75,000,000	25,700,000
Year 14	27,700,000	53,200,000	77,600,000	26,600,000
Year 15	28,700,000	55,100,000	80,300,000	27,500,000
Year 16	29,700,000	57,000,000	83,100,000	28,500,000
Year 17	30,700,000	59,000,000	86,000,000	29,500,000
Year 18	31,800,000	61,100,000	89,000,000	30,500,000
Year 19	32,900,000	63,200,000	92,100,000	31,600,000
Year 20	34,100,000	65,400,000	95,300,000	32,700,000
Year 21	35,300,000	67,700,000	98,600,000	33,800,000
Year 22	36,500,000	70,100,000	102,100,000	35,000,000
Year 23	37,800,000	72,600,000	105,700,000	36,200,000
Year 24	39,100,000	75,100,000	109,400,000	37,500,000
Year 25	40,500,000	77,700,000	113,200,000	38,800,000

Note: These figures reflect price increases of 3.5% annually, rounded to the nearest hundred thousand.

The costs of new plants and plant expansions depend on the year your company initiates construction (as shown in Table 3-3); however, ***the costs of new plant construction are subject to change (up or down) as the game progresses.*** The costs of all capital expenditure decisions (automation options, new plants, and plant expansions) show up in the calculations section of the plant decisions screen (the dark-shaded section of Exhibit 3-4). ***Payments for new plants and plant expansions are due the year the facilities are available for production (i.e. the year after being ordered).***

Labor productivity at new European or Asian plants starts out at 3,000 pairs per worker per year; the reject rate for new plants approximates 5% in the first year. In the case of plant expansions, labor productivity and reject rates correspond to those for the existing plant. Keep in mind that construction or expansion of plants takes 1 year. For example, a plant ordered in Year 11 comes on line ready for full production at the beginning of Year 12; an expansion ordered in Year 12 is available for full production at the beginning of Year 13. ***There is no limit on the number of times a plant can be expanded nor is there a limit on the absolute size of a given plant, but the maximum size of a plant expansion in any one year is 9 million pairs.*** You and your co-managers should analyze whether using overtime to increase production is cheaper or more expensive than adding new capacity. For instance, a company with 5,000,000 pairs of capacity that wants to boost production to 6,000,000 pairs may find that unit costs are lower producing at full 20% overtime rather than investing in another 1,000,000 pairs of plant capacity.

> ***REMINDER:*** *As was mentioned earlier, corporate overhead costs rise in stair-step fashion as the company's production capacity increases (not counting overtime capability).* ***Overhead charges will go up by $750,000 for each of the first 2 million pairs of capacity added past the current 3-million pair level, by $1,000,000 for each of the next two millions pairs added (up to a total capacity of 7,000,000 pairs), by $1,500,000 for each of the next 3 million pairs (up to 10 million pairs), and by $2,000,000 for each 1 million pairs of capacity over 10 million pairs.*** *These increases will occur in the year that new plant capacity comes on line. Overhead costs will decline in similar stair-step fashion if capacity additions are subsequently sold or permanently closed, but can never fall below the current $2,000,000 level.*

PLANT PURCHASES AND SALES. Instead of building new plant capacity and paying new-construction prices, you can purchase an entire plant or part of a plant (in multiples of 1,000,000 pairs) from a rival company. Alternatively, you can sell all or part of any plant (except Ohio) to a rival company. The price at which existing plant capacity is purchased/sold is negotiated by the buyer and seller, but the agreed-on price is ***subject to approval of your instructor or game administrator*** to ensure "arms-length" transactions and prevent "sweetheart deals." ***The Ohio plant cannot be sold*** — the Tebo family plans to exercise its first right of refusal to buy the property back in the event the plant is put up for sale or permanently shut. Your only options in Ohio are (1) to continue to operate it as is, trying to reduce operating costs and improve work force efficiency as best you can, (2) to invest in the various automation options available and otherwise make a concerted effort to get per pair costs down to a more competitive level, (3) to temporarily close the plant and operate it on an as needed basis, or (4) to permanently close it down and incur write-offs.

> ***Plant capacity purchase and sale agreements are subject to approval by your instructor / game administrator.***

> ***The Ohio plant cannot be expanded or sold.***

Any company that sells a plant ***below*** its undepreciated value (equal to net plant investment as shown on the manufacturing report) will realize an extraordinary loss; the loss will be reported on the company's income statement in the year plant ownership is transferred to the buyer (the beginning of the following year). Since the purchase/sale of plant capacity negotiated and approved in the Year 12 decision period becomes effective in Year 13, it is Year 13's net plant investment that is the basis for calculating extraordinary gains and losses.

If you negotiate a capacity sale or purchase with a rival company that is approved by your instructor/game administrator, ownership of the plant will be transferred on January 1 of the ***following year*** and the buyer will have full use of the plant capacity at that time. Plant capacity purchased from another company is treated as having a 20-year life and is depreciated at a 5% annual rate. The starting labor productivity of purchased plant capacity is 3000

> ***When plant capacity is purchased or sold, the ownership of the capacity and the cash payment are transferred at the beginning of the following year.***

pairs per worker per year; however, if the buyer already has a plant operating in that particular geographic region, worker productivity for the purchased capacity will be set at the same level as the buyer's present plant. For example, if in Year 14 Company A (which, let us say, operates a 2,000,000-pair plant in Texas) agrees to purchase Company B's 2,000,000-pair Texas plant, then in Year 15 Company A will have a 4,000,000-pair plant in Texas, and worker productivity at the expanded Texas plant will begin at the level otherwise prevailing at Company A's Texas plant. Also, all purchased plants are treated as having no automation option (in other words, the buyer of an existing plant obtains no benefit from any automation option that a purchased plant has been equipped with). However, if a buyer already has a plant operating in that same geographic area ***and*** if the buyer's existing plant has an automation option in place, then the automation benefits of the buyer's existing plant will automatically be extended to the purchased capacity.

All plant capacity purchased must remain in the area where built — you cannot buy all or part of another company's Texas plant and move it to Asia; it must remain in Texas. To execute a capacity purchase or sale, ***first get approval on the price from your instructor or game administrator***, then enter the approved price (in thousands) and the amount of capacity being bought/sold (in thousands) in the appropriate location column.

As you can see from looking at the calculations section of Exhibit 3-4, when you finish making entries on the plant decisions screen, you are provided with a recap of the plant capacity available next year as well as the capital expenditures scheduled at each plant and any extraordinary gains or losses associated with your decisions.

TEMPORARY PLANT SHUTDOWNS. Occasionally market conditions may make it advisable to drastically cut production levels in one or more plants, perhaps even to zero. To ***temporarily*** shut down production operations at a particular plant, all you have to do is enter a zero for pairs to be manufactured on the manufacturing decisions screen and a zero for number of workers employed on the labor decisions screen. Variable costs at the temporarily shut plant will then be zero for the year but your company will still incur full-year depreciation charges and 25% of normal maintenance costs. Company accountants will allocate the fixed costs associated with temporary plant shutdowns to the manufacturing cost of goods available for sale in the region. When you and your co-managers decide to reopen the plant (it can remain "temporarily shut" for as many years as desired), ***worker productivity will resume at about 90% of the worker productivity value that prevailed in the last year of plant operation***.

> ***Upon re-opening a plant that has been idle for a year or more, worker productivity at the plant will resume at about 90% of the productivity value that prevailed in the last year the plant was operated.***

PRIVATE-LABEL MARKETING DECISIONS

If you and your co-managers elect to enter bids to supply private-label footwear to chain discounters, there are three decisions to be made annually: (1) how many pairs to offer to chain store buyers, (2) what price to bid, and, (3) in the event your company's bid price is too high to sell all of the pairs offered, whether to have the Memphis warehouse staff convert a designated number of unsold private-label pairs to branded pairs (by affixing an adhesive-backed, non-removable sticker with the company's logo on each shoe and then packaging pairs in the company's distinctive boxes). The present cost of converting private-label pairs to branded pairs is $0.25 per pair, but this cost is subject to change in future years.

> ***Bids from companies whose private-label warehouse stock do not meet buyer specs (currently has a quality rating of 50 or greater and a model availability of 50 or greater) are automatically thrown out. Bid prices must also be at least $2.50 below the average wholesale price in North America for branded footwear to be considered.***

One issue min product range min quality
private 50 cable 120
should make only one quality shoe in a specific factory
Price is the main factor
can convert from private to brand

The private-label decision entries are shown in Exhibit 3-5. Currently, private-label retailers require a quality rating of at least 50 and model availability of 50 of all bidders (these specifications are subject to change as the game progresses).

Exhibit 3-5: Private-Label Marketing Decisions Screen

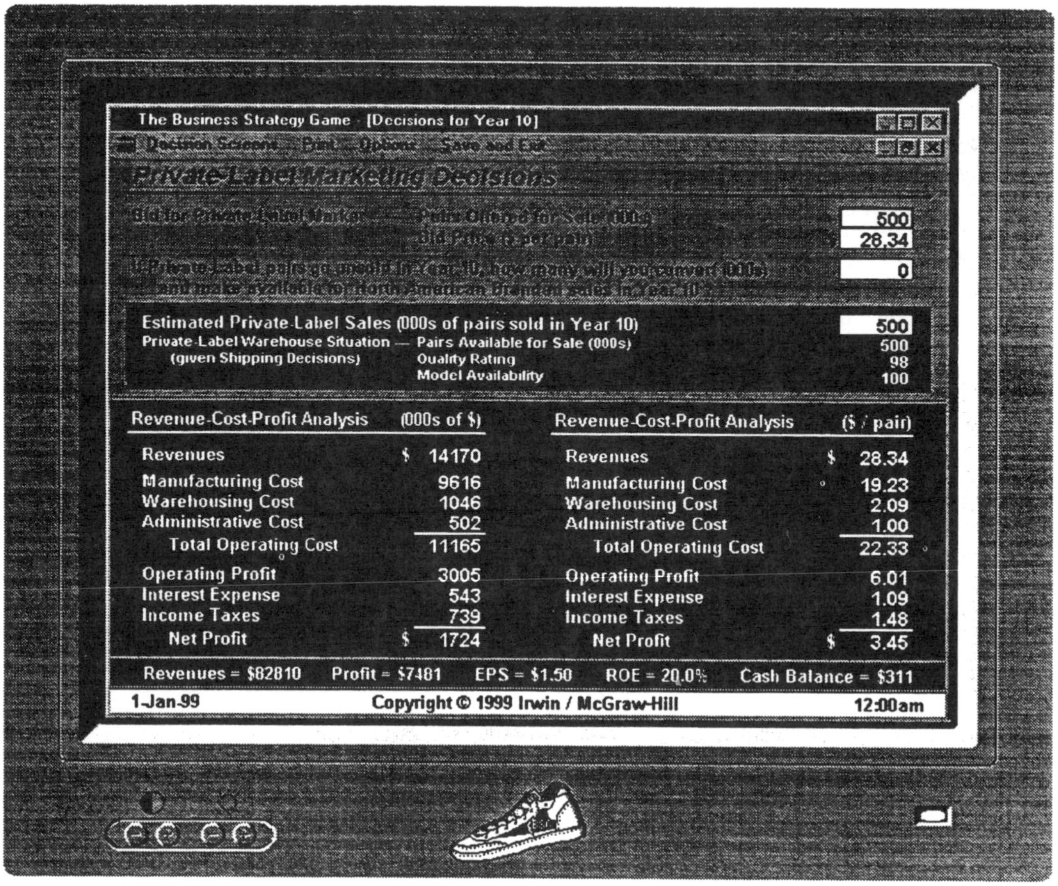

Bids from companies which meet all buyer specifications are awarded in 50,000-pair lots, starting with the lowest-priced bidder and then accepting each ascending bid until either buyer demand is satisfied or all qualified bids are accepted, whichever occurs first. If you decide to bid for private-label sales, (1) enter a bid price down to the penny and (2) indicate the quantity your company is willing to offer at that price — 50,000, 100,000, 150,000, 200,000 pairs and on up (but always in lots of 50,000). Depending on the amount chain stores are buying, the price bids of rivals, and the various quantities offered, your company may sell all of the pairs offered to private-label buyers, some of the pairs offered, or nothing.

> ***If two or more companies bid the same price, the tie goes to the bidder with the highest private-label quality rating; if both price and quality are the same, model availability serves as the second tie-breaker.***

Since the outcome of the private-label bidding is known early in the year, all or some of the private-label pairs offered but not sold to chain discounters may, at management's direction, be re-branded, stocked in the branded section of the Memphis warehouse, and made available to North America retail dealers at the branded price. If you want to immediately direct some or all unsold pairs to the branded market, simply enter the unsold amount you want converted (in thousands of pairs) in the appropriate cell on the decision screen. You can determine the impact of converting unsold pairs on branded quality by entering a what-if forecast for private-label sales that assumes the conversion will occur and then observing the resulting change in branded quality on the branded marketing decisions screen. ***If you prefer, unsold private-label pairs can be allowed to remain in private-label inventory and you can try to sell them in the following year's bidding process. Storage costs for unsold pairs and the standard 5-point quality rating reduction for unsold pairs will apply.***

The final entry on the private-label marketing screen is your estimate of the number of private-label pairs you will sell at the bid price. You can gauge the downside impact on company performance of not selling the full amount offered by entering lesser-amount what-if forecasts and observing the resulting changes in revenue, profit, earnings per share, and ROE at the bottom of the screen. Utilizing the other calculations provided in the bottom section of this screen, you can also see how sensitive costs and profitability are to different sales volumes.

BRANDED MARKETING DECISIONS

Decisions regarding branded marketing have a far-reaching impact on the strength of your company's competitive effort relative to rivals and the attractiveness of your company's branded footwear as compared to competing brands. The Year 10 decisions of prior management are shown on the branded marketing decisions screen in Exhibit 3-6.

Exhibit 3-6: BRANDED MARKETING DECISIONS SCREEN

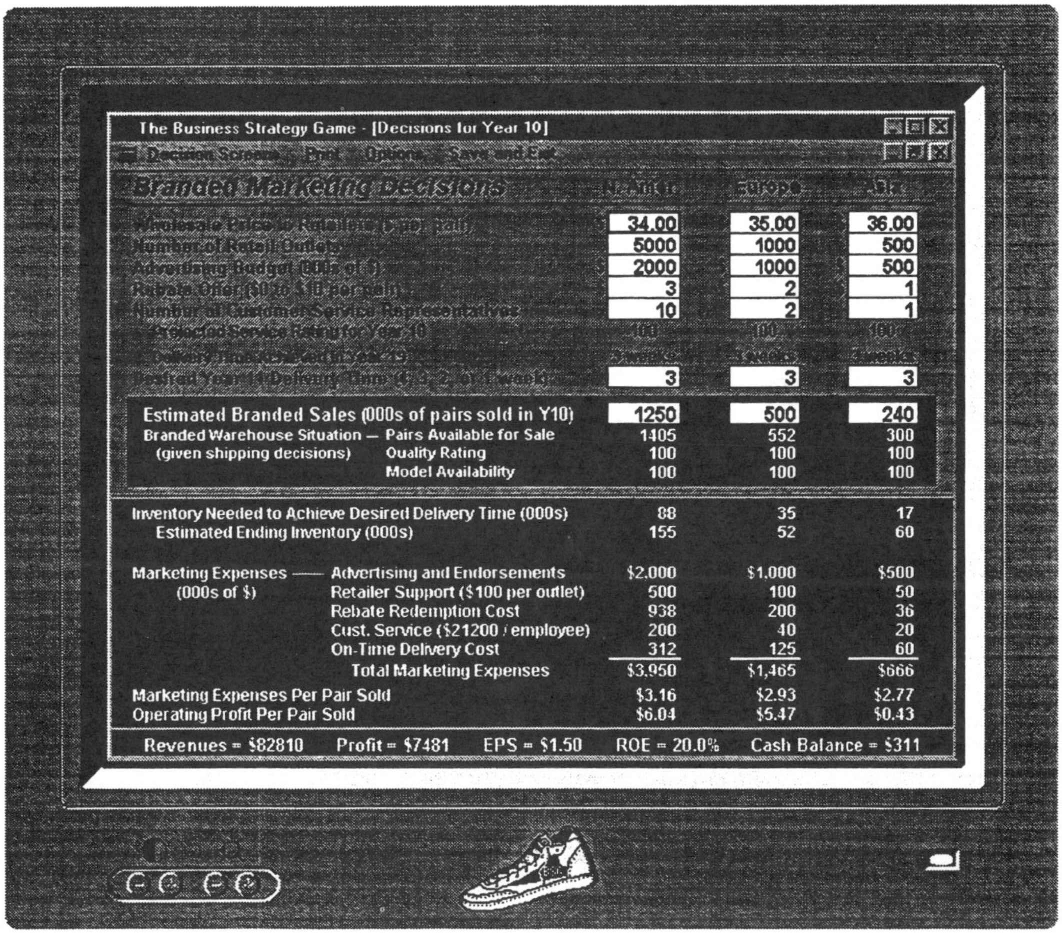

Price
NB Advertising (Diff, best cost)
Rebate offer
Customer representatives
Delivery time: shorter time period more cost, more stock

PRICING. The maximum price you can charge per branded pair is $99.99. There is no limit on how much you can raise or lower price from one year to the next. If you do not wish to sell any pairs in a particular geographic area, simply enter a zero price for that area and cut back your marketing efforts to zero (or to whatever amounts you wish to go ahead and spend anyway). As discussed in Section 1, your company's wholesale price relative to competitors is a key determinant of market share. but low price alone is usually insufficient to assure outselling rivals by a hefty margin.

RETAIL OUTLETS. The upper limit on the number of retail outlets you can have in an area is 99,999 (which should prove more than ample). There are diminishing marginal benefits to having progressively more retail outlets than rivals. However, if you have no outlets in an area, branded sales will be zero — consumers have to have a place to go to buy your footwear. The entries for retail outlets represent the total number ***(these entries are not made in thousands)***. If you decide you want 6,000 North American dealers, then enter 6000 (not 6). At present, retailer support costs equal $100 for each retail outlet the company has in North America, Europe, and Asia, but this cost is subject to change as the game progresses.

ADVERTISING EXPENDITURES. Your company can gain a competitive advantage over rivals in capturing market share by outspending them on advertising. Of course, you have to be careful that greater advertising expenditures don't get costs out of line or reduce overall profitability — there are diminishing marginal benefits from outspending rivals on advertising by a wider and wider margin. Enter all advertising expenditures in thousands of dollars (for example, enter 2500 to spend $2,500,000 on advertising).

CUSTOMER REBATES. Offering sizable rebates to consumers can also be a source of competitive advantage. If you elect to employ promotional rebates, you have ten options ranging from as little as $1 to as much as $10 per pair. All rebate offers must be in round dollars. Deciding against use of a rebate is always an option. Different rebates can be used in each geographic market. Customer response to rebates is a function of the size of the rebate (rebates in the $8 to $10 range will generate a more than proportional market share response compared to $3 to $5 rebates) and the amount by which your company's rebate is above/below the average rebate in that geographic market. ***Since all buyers will not mail in the rebate coupon, the per pair cost of a promotional rebate is below the face value of the coupon*** *(see the table).*

Rebate Offer	*Redemption Rate*	*Cost Per Pair Sold*
$1	*15%*	*$0.15*
2	*20*	*0.40*
3	*25*	*0.75*
4	*30*	*1.20*
5	*35*	*1.75*
6	*40*	*2.40*
7	*45*	*3.15*
8	*50*	*4.00*
9	*55*	*4.95*
10	*60*	*6.00*

CUSTOMER SERVICE REPRESENTATIVES. One customer service representative can satisfactorily service 500 retail outlets; ratios above 500 to 1 will penalize your service rating and ratios smaller than 500 to 1 will boost your service rating. The costs of supporting the work of one customer service rep were $20,000 in Year 10 and will escalate at the rate of 6% annually (Year 11 costs will be $21,200 per rep in all geographic areas). There are diminishing marginal benefits to progressively smaller outlet-to-service-rep ratios; there's no benefit to a ratio smaller than 25:1.

DELIVERY TIME. Retailers consider a delivery time of 4 weeks as "satisfactory." Shorter delivery times will boost your company's service rating. Currently, 3-week delivery entails a cost of $0.25 per pair, 2-week delivery costs $0.75 per pair, and 1-week delivery costs $1.50 per pair. However, the more models in your product line and the shorter the delivery time you try to achieve, the bigger the inventory your company must have in each distribution center to be able to completely fill retailer orders for various sizes and styles. The first two lines in the calculations section of the branded marketing decisions screen (the bottom section of Exhibit 3-

6) provide the requisite inventory status information — (1) how big your inventories need to be to meet the desired delivery times, given the number of models available in each warehouse and (2) the projected ending inventories (given your forecast of branded sales). If your estimated ending inventory levels are below the required levels, you will have to decide whether to lengthen the desired delivery time, to increase production and build up warehouse inventories to the needed levels, or live with the prospects of a lower service rating for next year. Remember that inventory storage costs rise progressively as unsold finished goods inventory rises — per pair inventory storage costs ***at each warehouse*** are $0.25 for the first 500,000 pairs in unsold inventory, $0.50 per pair for the next 250,000 pairs, $0.75 per pair on all pairs between 750,000 and 1,000,000 pairs, $1.00 per pair on all pairs between 1,000,000 and 1,250,000 pairs, and $1.50 on each unsold pair in excess of 1,250,000 pairs.

> ***Failure to achieve the needed inventory levels will delay shipments to retailers beyond the desired delivery time and result in a lower-than-expected service rating in the following year.***

THE WHAT-IF SALES ESTIMATES. After you have entered tentative decisions for selling prices, advertising, retail dealers, customer rebates, customer service staff, and delivery times, you and your co-managers will need to agree on an estimate of the number of pairs that can be sold given the prices, product quality, model availability, and marketing effort being made in each geographic region. In Year 11 you know that branded footwear demand will ***average*** 1,450,000 pairs in North America, 600,000 pairs in Europe, and 350,000 pairs in Asia. By out-competing rival companies in a given geographic area, your company can achieve sales volumes exceeding these averages. While taking some market share away from less competitive brands is not particularly hard, your company's product attractiveness and competitive effort will have to be ***significantly*** stronger than rival companies to achieve sales volumes that are 20% to 30% or more above the market averages. It will take progressively lower prices and progressively greater product differentiation to win enough market share away from rivals to outsell them by 50%, 75%, 100%, or more. It is possible but not easy to double, maybe triple, your company's market share at the expense of rivals. However, such successes may prove short-lived because rivals can be expected to retaliate in the following year by upping their competitive effort and trying to regain some of their market share losses.

NB

THE DEMAND FORECASTING MODEL

To forecast the number of branded pairs your company can anticipate selling in each branded geographic region, you should use the Demand Forecasting Model. When you click on this menu option, the demand forecasting screen will load and appear in a few seconds – it is shown in Exhibit 3-7.

In the first block on the screen are three columns of numbers and entries for each of the three branded markets. The first column merely records the current entries you've made on the branded marketing decisions screen (as concerns retail outlets, advertising, rebates, and wholesale selling price) and the other current factors that shape your company's overall competitive effort (number of models, product quality, customer service rating, and image rating) to win sales and market share in North America, Europe, and Asia. When you first arrive at the demand forecasting screen, these same values already appear in the cells in the "what-if" marketing effort column (the second column). In the third column (labeled Industry Average Marketing Effort), you will have to enter projections of what the industry average competitive effort will be — in other words, you must enter your best estimate of what the average number of models offered will be in the upcoming year for all companies competing in that geographic market, then put in an estimate of what the average quality rating of all pairs available for sale in that geographic market will be, and so on. This requires making judgments about whether competitors, on average, will increase/decrease the number of models in their product line, increase/decrease the quality of their branded shoe offering, increase/decrease their advertising levels, and so forth. Then in the block below all these entries, you have to tell the computer what the forecasted ***total*** demand in each market (in thousands of pairs) is expected to be. For example, in Year 11 you know from page 8 that the average number of branded pairs expected to be sold in North America is 1,450,000 pairs; if there are 10 companies in your industry, total market demand in North America is forecasted to be 14,500,000 pairs. Hence you would enter 14,500 in the cell for North America. In the next row, you must enter how many companies you expect to be competing in each of the three branded markets.

Exhibit 3-7: Demand Forecasting Screen

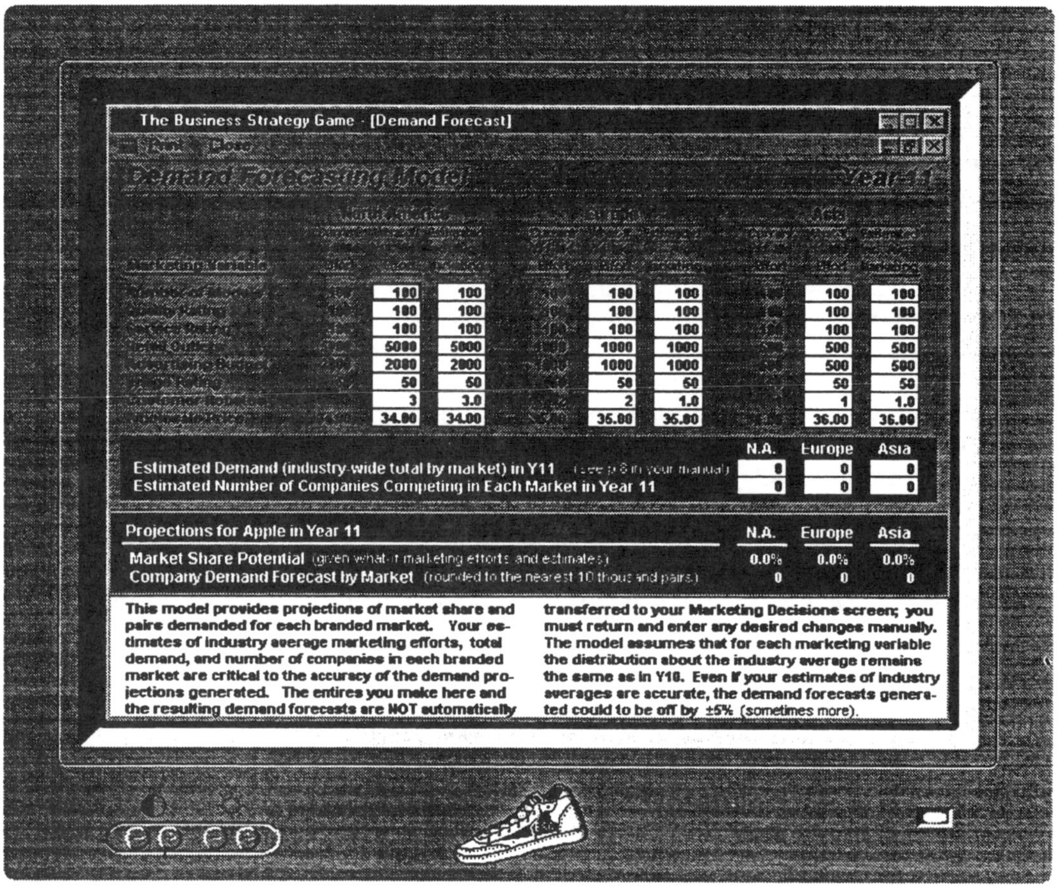

When you've entered values for all of the cells, the demand forecasting model provides you with ***projections*** of your company's market share and how many pairs your company can expect to sell — the model's projections are not guarantees. The projections may deviate from the realized sales and market shares for three reasons: (1) your estimates of one or more of the industry averages (and thus the degree of competition from rivals) may prove to be too high or too low, (2) several rivals may significantly alter their competitive efforts in ways that cause the projections to be off target, and (3) the number of companies competing in each market may turn out to be more or less than you estimate. ***Normally***, the projected sales volumes will prove accurate within ±5% of the number of pairs actually sold, ***provided your estimates of the number of competitors and the upcoming year's industry averages are on target.***

Using the Demand Forecasting Model for What-Iffing. The demand forecasting screen provides you and your co-managers with valuable what-iffing capability. If you and your co-managers are in doubt about what industry average values to use as the basis for your demand forecast, then one good approach is to run worst-case and best-case scenarios. The worst-case scenario entails entering fairly strong increases in the industry averages (which signals stronger competition in the marketplace than previously) and observing the resulting downside impact on your projected sales volumes and market share. A best-case scenario involves entering little or no increase in the industry averages (which signals not much change in rivals' overall competitive effort) and observing the upside impact on your company's projected sales volumes and market shares. The worst-case and best-case projections provide a ***range*** in which your actual sales volumes and market shares should fall.

If the projected market share and sales volumes are below the levels you would like (or if they exceed what you are able to supply), go back to the "what-if marketing effort" column for your company and watch what happens to the projected number of pairs sold when you raise/lower the number of models, increase/decrease quality, spend more/less on advertising, increase/decrease the wholesale price, and so on. By playing around with different combinations of prices, models, quality, rebates, advertising, and so on, you can get a pretty good handle on what level of prices and marketing effort will be required to achieve the desired market share and sales volume in each of the three branded markets. When your and your co-managers reach a consensus on the what-if entries for your company (models, quality, retail outlets, rebates, advertising, and so on) that you believe will be needed to achieve the target sales volumes and market shares, ***given the anticipated competition from rivals that are reflected in the industry averages you have entered***, then you should return to the other screens and revise your decision entries accordingly. Use the projected sales volumes provided by the demand forecasting model as the basis for entering the what-if sales forecast values on the branded marketing decision screen.

In the years ahead, you'll find that the demand forecasting screen provides valuable guidance in forecasting sales and in helping you and your co-managers choose what price to charge and what branded marketing effort to employ. It is an especially good what-iffing tool.

THE INVENTORY LIQUIDATION OPTION

There may be occasions in future years when your company unexpectedly builds up unwanted inventories of unsold pairs in one or more distribution centers. This can occur because of excess production capacity in the industry relative to market demand or perhaps because your company has been outcompeted by rival companies. In such cases, you and your co-managers may wish to consider unloading some or all of the unwanted inventory at liquidation prices rather than contend with the problems of having to market them.

Exhibit 3-8: INVENTORY LIQUIDATION DIALOG BOX

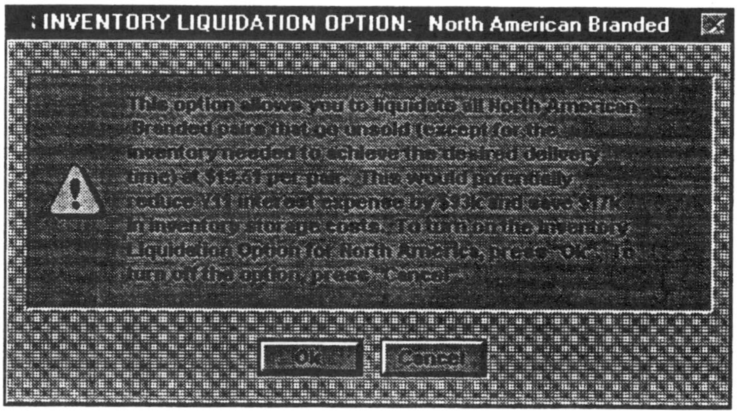

stock level too high : sell bellow cost

When you select the menu option for inventory liquidation, a dialog box will appear (see the example in Exhibit 3-8 above) explaining the option and showing the liquidation price that inventory liquidators are willing to pay for your excess pairs. It also provides you with an estimate of the potential savings on storage costs and inventory financing. The liquidation price will typically be ***below*** the cost incurred to manufacture the pairs and will not cover any shipping, import tariff, marketing, administrative, or interest costs that might be associated with the inventory to be liquidated. Therefore, you and your co-managers should use this option sparingly — usually, only in instances when selling the excess inventory through normal channels is impractical and presents too big a market hurdle.

If the liquidation terms are acceptable, simply click the "OK" button to accept the liquidation offer or click the "Cancel" button to reject the option. When you accept the liquidation offer, a check mark (√) will appear on the menu next to the warehouse in which the excess inventory to be liquidated is housed.

BIDS FOR NEW CELEBRITY ENDORSEMENT CONTRACTS

Twelve new celebrity sports figures from all over the world have indicated their willingness to wear a company's athletic footwear and endorse its brand in company ads if the fee they are paid is sufficiently attractive. All of the available sports personalities have hired agents to represent them in a competitive bidding process to decide whose brand they will endorse. The screen shown in Exhibit 3-9 provides the information needed to participate in the bid process if you and your co-managers are interested. Contract bids for three well-known sports celebrities will take place in Year 11; the remaining nine celebrities will be bid for in upcoming years according to the schedule shown in the next to last column of Exhibit 3-9.

Exhibit 3-9: CELEBRITY ENDORSEMENT BID SCREEN

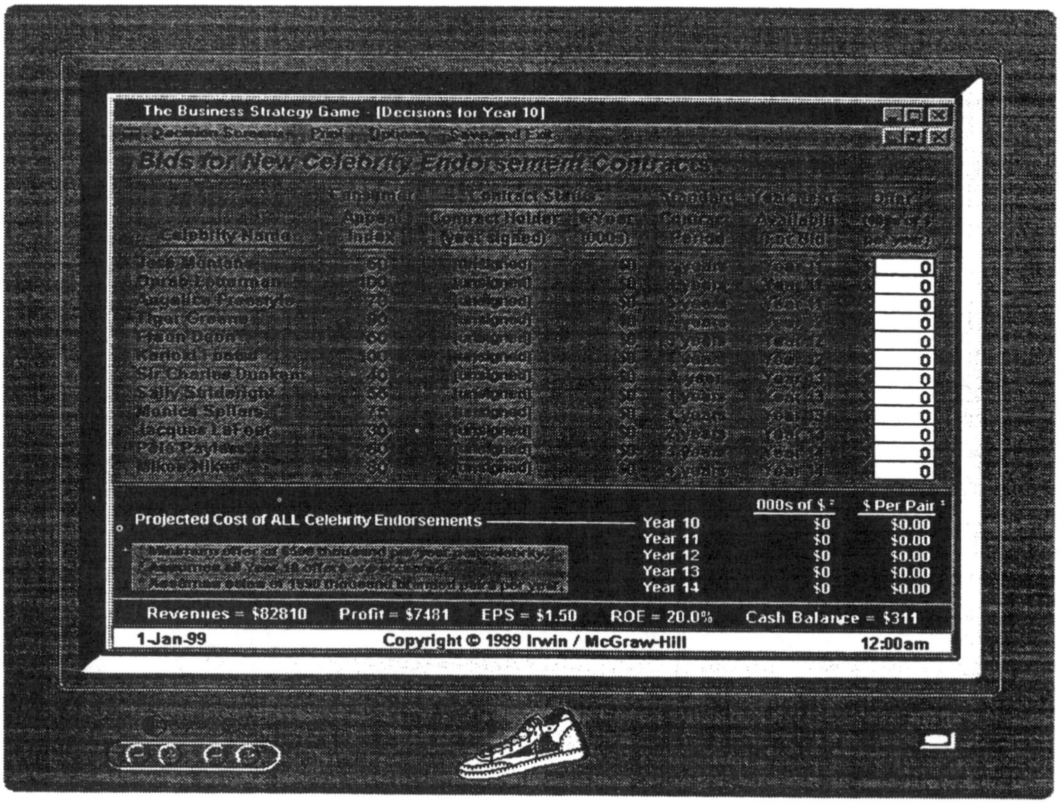

highest price wins

What are you going to do with the person, cost a lot

must be able to afford them

While all of the twelve celebrities are known worldwide, their degree of consumer recognition and influence varies according to the ***consumer appeal index*** shown on the screen — the endorsement influence of each celebrity has the same market impact in each geographic region (for reasons of simplicity). A celebrity with a consumer appeal index of 100 will have twice as much market impact as one with an index of 50. The impact of signing several high profile celebrities has a strong positive impact on your company's brand image rating — celebrity endorsements carry a 40% weight in the International Footwear Federation's image rating calculation. The higher the sum of the consumer appeal indexes of the celebrity endorsers your company signs, the higher your company's overall brand image rating and the greater the branded sales volume that can be achieved (other things being equal). There is no limit on the number of celebrities that can be signed by a particular company. However, there is a rapidly diminishing market impact associated with signing additional celebrities once the sum of their consumer appeal indexes rises above 400. Whether the incremental sales and profits contributed by a celebrity endorser are sufficient to cover the contract fees paid will, of course, depend on how high you have to bid to win the celebrity's endorsement. There is credible market research indicating that the value of celebrity endorsements in the athletic footwear business will have a positive bottom-line payoff if the contract fees that have to be paid to win endorsements are not unreasonably high.

The standard contract periods vary by celebrity as you can see from the exhibit. All contract offers are based on so many dollars to be paid to the celebrity each year of the contract; celebrities will sign with the company making the highest offer (subject to a required minimum of $500,000 per year). In the event of ties in the highest offer, the celebrity will sign with the company whose celebrity endorsers have the ***lowest*** combined consumer appeal indexes (if the high bidders have celebrity endorsers with the same combined consumer appeal indexes, the celebrity will sign with the company having the ***lowest*** overall image rating). The preference of celebrity endorsers to sign with companies having a weaker lineup of endorsers reflects their belief that this will give them greater overall exposure as the company's principal spokesperson. The potential for ties argues for odd-number contract offers. Your company will incur a cost of $100,000 for each bid it submits for a celebrity's services; this cost is subject to change as the game progresses

If your company is the winning bidder for the services of a particular celebrity, the celebrity will be available in the year FOLLOWING your winning bid and you will begin to pay the celebrity's annual contract cost in the year FOLLOWING your winning bid — no costs other than the bid fee are incurred in the year of the bid.

FINANCIAL DECISIONS

Financial decisions made by prior management in Year 10 are shown on the financial decisions screen (Exhibit 3-10). How you and your co-managers handle the financing of company operations has a big impact on the company's bond rating, the interest rates your company pays on new bond issues and short-term loans, the company's return on equity investment, and the company's stock price.

INTEREST RATES ON BONDS AND SHORT-TERM LOANS. Your company's bond rating is a function of the company's debt-to-asset ratio and the number of times which operating profit exceeds annual interest expenses (commonly referred to as the times-interest-earned coverage ratio). The methodology used by securities analysts to determine company bond ratings is programmed on the company disk, allowing you to obtain projections of the bond rating based on current year decisions and projected company performance — see the next-to-last line in the calculations section on the finance decisions screen. There are seven bond ratings, and the interest rates your company pays on new bond issues and short-term loans is tied to the bond rating as presented in Table 3-4 on the following page.

source of money: short/long bonds shares   Neg cost: short term load high interest rate

Interest rate: depends on bond rating

Table 3-4: INTEREST RATES AND ADJUSTMENT FACTORS

Bond Rating	Interest Rate on New Bond Issues	Interest Rate on Short-Term Loans
AAA	7.50%* or as announced	7.50%* or as announced
AA	AAA rate plus 0.50%	Prime rate plus 0.50%
A	AAA rate plus 1.25%	Prime rate plus 1.25%
BBB	AAA rate plus 2.00%	Prime rate plus 2.00%
BB	AAA rate plus 3.00%	Prime rate plus 3.00%
B	AAA rate plus 5.00%	Prime rate plus 5.00%
C	AAA rate plus 8.00%	Prime rate plus 8.00%

* *The 7.5% rate will prevail for future years unless modified in some fashion described by your instructor/game administrator.*

SHORT-TERM LOANS. The company's agreement with its consortium of North American, European, and Asian banks states that ***management has discretionary authority to borrow any amount on a short term basis up to $100 million, provided the company's projected bond rating and debt status does not become alarming to creditors.*** The interest rate paid on short-term loans is tied to the company's current bond rating — for example, a short-term loan taken out in Year 11 carries an interest rate based on the Year 11 bond rating. All short-term loans are repaid the year after they are taken out, but amounts needed to repay prior short-term loans can be financed with a new short-term loan at the prevailing interest rate. You will need to be careful about the amount of debt your company incurs in the form of long-term bonds and short-term loans. Past a debt-to-assets ratio of 50%, the company's bond rating will deteriorate sharply unless the times-interest-earned coverage ratio is quite high. ***Once your company's bond rating reaches C (the lowest rating), your company may be denied access to additional short-term loans or bonds unless additional shares of stock are issued and the debt-to asset ratio improves enough to satisfy creditors.***

COMMON STOCK ISSUES. It is very likely in financing the company's growth that additional shares of common stock will have to be issued. Investor interest in the company has been high enough that you can count on being able to sell additional shares and raise new equity capital. ***New shares of common stock are issued at the prevailing market price less a discount based on the percentage dilution.*** For example, issuing 10% more shares will entail an issue price per new share roughly 10% below the prevailing price appearing in the most recent issue of the Footwear Industry Report. ***When you enter the number of shares (in thousands) to be issued, the discounted issue price will be displayed beside the new stock issue entry in the projected cash inflows listing (on the left side of the calculations section of the screen). The company's board of directors has voted to limit you and your co-managers to a maximum of $200 million in stock sales in any one year — this $200 million annual limit will prevail throughout the game.*** The following example takes you through the cash flow and balance sheet implications of stock issues:

> Assume that in Year 11 the company decides to raise capital by issuing 1 million shares of stock and that the discounted issue price turns out to be $12 per share. The 1,000,000-share stock issue will then generate $12 million in cash (1 million shares × $12 per share) available for use in Year 11. In the stockholders' equity portion of the balance sheet, the Common Stock account will increase by $1 million ($1 par value × 1 million shares issued), and the Additional Stockholders' Capital account will increase by $11 million [($12 issue price − $1 par value) × 1 million shares issued].

BOND ISSUES. All bonds are issued for a 10-year term. The interest rates on each long-term bond issue will correspond to the company's bond rating as of the prior year — in other words, a bond issued in Year 12 carries an interest rate based on the Year 11 bond rating. ***Your company is limited to a maximum of 10 bond issues (2 of which have already been used up by prior management) and to a maximum of $99,999,000 per new bond issue.***

Exhibit 3-10: FINANCIAL DECISIONS SCREEN

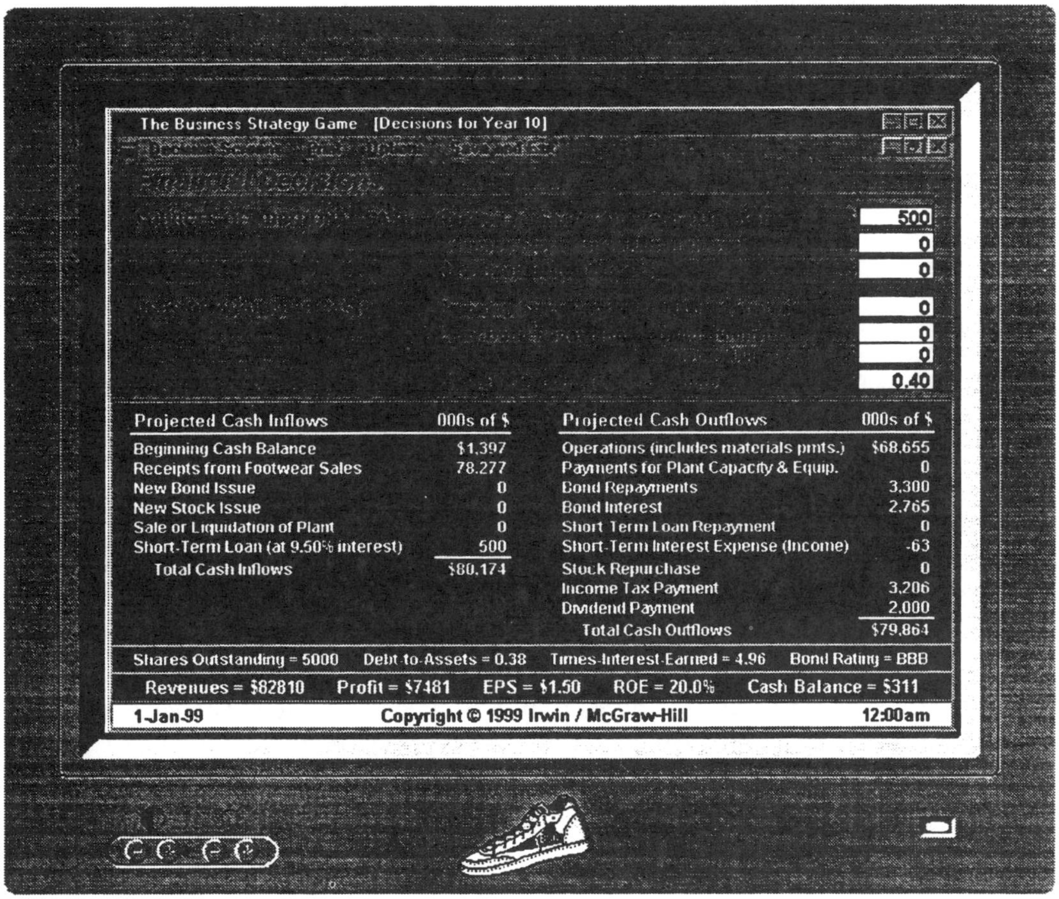

It is common practice for bondholders to require a 2.0 coverage ratio as security against excessive use of long-term debt. ***Should your company's time-interest-earned ratio fall below 2.0 in a particular year, the company will be barred from floating a new bond issue in the following year.*** For example, if the company's interest coverage ratio drops to 1.8 in Year 12, no new bonds can be issued in Year 13. If the interest coverage ratio rises in Year 13 to 2.0 or greater, your company will regain access to the bond market in Year 14. Also, ***if your company's projected bond rating falls deep into the C range, your company may be denied access to further debt even if the times-interest-earned ratio is above 2.0*** unless stockholders put up additional equity in the form of a new stock issue — you will get a screen prompt when this condition is reached. Consequently, ***you and your co-managers are well-advised to observe prudent financial management practices and avoid irresponsible or foolish financial "wheeling and dealing."*** The principal on 10-year bonds is repaid annually in equal installments; interest on the outstanding principal is paid annually.

> *To qualify for a new bond issue, your company's times-interest-earned ratio must exceed 2.0 in the year preceding a new issue*

COMMON STOCK RETIREMENT. If you and your co-managers wish to retire outstanding shares by repurchasing them from investors, then you may buy them back at a price that escalates above the prevailing price according to percentage of shares being retired. In other words, ***stock buybacks drive up the price of the remaining shares; the bigger the buyback, the higher the repurchase price.*** When you enter the number of shares (in thousands) to be repurchased on the finance decisions screen, the computer will display a message indicating the buyback price beside the stock repurchase entry in the projected cash outflows listing on the bottom right of the screen. Stock repurchases can be paid for by using cash on hand, taking out short-term loans, issuing a new bond, or even cutting the dividend. However, the Board of Directors has decreed that the company will have no fewer than 3,000,000 shares outstanding; hence, ***you cannot repurchase shares in an amount that will bring the number of shares outstanding below the 3,000,000-share minimum.*** The following example takes you through the cash flow and balance sheet implications of stock retirement:

> Assume that in Year 11 the company decides to retire 1 million shares of outstanding stock at a buyback price of $18.50. The 1,000,000-share stock retirement will require $18.5 million in cash ($18.50 per share × 1 million shares retired). In the stockholders' equity section of the balance sheet, the Common Stock account will decrease by $1 million ($1 par value × 1 million shares retired) and the Additional Stockholders' Capital account will decrease by $17.5 million [($18.50 repurchase price − $1 par value) × 1 million shares retired].

Once the Additional Stockholders' Capital account balance reaches zero, company accountants treat the cost of stock repurchases as a deduction from Retained Earnings (except for the $1 par value deducted from the Common Stock account). ***The cost of shares repurchased cannot be so great as to throw your company into a negative retained earnings position. Once the amount of accumulated retained earnings showing on the balance sheet reaches zero, all further stock repurchases will be automatically denied.***[1]

EARLY BOND REPAYMENT. You can retire all or part of any outstanding bond early if you wish, but there is a 2% prepayment penalty on the early retirement amount. To use the early bond payment decision option, simply enter the bond number (1 through 10 — see Note 2 on the balance sheet) that you wish to make an ***extra*** payment on, and enter the amount of the ***extra*** payment. The 2% prepayment penalty will be calculated by the computer immediately upon an early bond repayment entry, and automatically charged to bond interest for the year.

CASH BALANCES. The company's arrangement with its banks calls for the banks to pay the company interest on any positive cash balance the company has in its checking account at the beginning of each year. The agreed-upon interest rate is set at three points below the prevailing prime interest rate. At present (unless announced otherwise), the prime rate is 7.5%; thus the money market rate paid on cash balances is 4.5%. If you and your co-managers should at any time fail to maintain a year-end cash balance of zero or greater, the banks will automatically issue your company a short-term loan in an amount sufficient to bring your checking account balance up to zero. The interest rate charged on the ***entire amount of short-term borrowing that year*** will be ***2% above the regular rate*** — in other words, if your bond rating entitles your company to a short-term interest rate of 8.25%, then the penalty rate in the case of an automatic bank loan would be 10.25% on the entire loan amount. Overdrawing your checking account is costly and should be avoided.

> ***Computer-generated short-term loans carry a 2% interest rate penalty over and above the regular interest rate.***

[1] *Keep in mind here that retained earnings are* ***not*** *cash and cannot be used to pay for anything. All the cash your company has is shown on the cash flow report. The accumulated retained earnings amount shown on the balance sheet is nothing but an accounting summation of the after-tax profits the company has earned over all its years of operation that have not been paid out to stockholders in the form of dividends.*

DIVIDENDS. The size of the company's annual dividend is a significant matter to stockholders, especially the three co-founders who depend on their annual dividend checks as a primary source of income. Increases or decreases in the dividend are reflected immediately in the stock price. It is your decision henceforth whether to continue the present $0.40 annual dividend, whether to raise it and how often, or whether to cut it.

In Year 10, the company earned $1.50 per share after taxes (as shown in the bottom calc section of Exhibit 3-11) and paid out $0.40 per share in dividends. With total earnings of $7,481,000 and total dividend payments of $2,000,000 ($0.40 per share × 5,000,000 shares outstanding), it follows that both accumulated retained earnings and total stockholders' equity in Year 10 increased by $5,479,000 ($7,481,000 – $2,000,000 = $5,479,000). If you declare a dividend that is higher than the current year's earnings, the accumulated retained earnings balance (and also total stockholders' equity) will decrease. ***Under no circumstances will you be allowed to declare a dividend if the company's accumulated retained earnings balance is negative or a dividend that would cause the company's accumulated retained earnings balance to become negative.*** Otherwise, the Board of Directors will approve whatever decision you recommend on dividends.

> *Paying a dividend below EPS raises total stockholder equity in the enterprise and, thus, has a direct impact on ROE.*

STOCK PRICE. At the end of Year 10, your company's stock price was $15 per share. Whether your company's stock price goes up or down as the game progresses is a function of:

1. ***The company's revenue growth*** (as measured by the compound growth rate of revenues since Year 10) — faster rates of revenue growth tend to push the stock price up.
2. ***The growth trend in the company's earnings per share*** (as compared to the Year 10 starting base of $1.50 per share) — higher growth rates in EPS will cause the stock price to rise significantly. Investors have decided that the trend in the company's earnings growth is best reflected by the compound rate of growth between average EPS for the most recent three years and the Year 10 EPS base of $1.50 per share.
3. ***The growth trend in dividends per share*** (as compared to the Year 10 starting base of $0.40 per share) — higher rates of dividend growth (as measured by the compound rate of growth between the average dividend per share for the most recent three years and the Year 10 base of $0.40 per share) will have a positive impact on the stock price.
4. ***Year-to-year changes in earnings per share*** — the bigger the year-to-year change in EPS (up or down), the bigger the impact on the year-to-year change in the stock price (up or down).
5. ***Year-to-year changes in the annual dividend*** — whether the dividend is increased, decreased, or left unchanged and the size of any increase or decrease. Annual dividend increases of a dependable size have a stronger positive effect than intermittent increases.
6. Whether ***the company's dividend payout ratio*** (defined as current dividends per share as a % of current earnings per share) exceeds 100% — paying a dividend that exceeds EPS has a depressing effect on the stock price, since it impairs cash flow and is unsustainable.
7. ***The company's bond rating*** — higher bond ratings have a positive effect on the stock price because they signal a stronger financial condition.
8. ***The annual rate of return earned on stockholders' equity*** — higher rates of return signal a more profitable use of investors' capital and have a positive impact on the stock price.

> *Your company's stock price is a function of 8 factors.*

Of these eight factors, the growth trends in earnings per share and dividends per share have the biggest impact on stock price. The year-to-year change in EPS has the third biggest impact. The rate of return on equity investment is the fourth most significant factor. The dividend payout ratio has virtually no impact ***unless*** the company fails to earn the dividend and the payout ratio exceeds 100%. The other factors are of intermediate importance.

EXECUTIVE COMPENSATION DECISIONS (OPTIONAL SCREEN)

At some juncture in the game, a ninth decision screen involving executive compensation may come into play — see Exhibit 3-11. This option involves deciding how much to compensate each member of the company's management team and the awarding of stock bonuses to individual managers. If and when use of this decision screen is activated by the instructor/game administrator, the automatic 5% annual increase in executive compensation will cease; you and your co-managers will have to decide on salaries and stock bonus awards for each team member. The compensation of each co-manager may be equal or unequal. While a good case can be made that salaries and stock bonus awards should be based on the relative performance and contribution of each co-manager, the allocations to each team member will be left for you and your co-managers to work out among yourselves (subject to any guidelines established by your instructor/game administrator).

Exhibit 3-11: EXECUTIVE COMPENSATION DECISIONS SCREEN

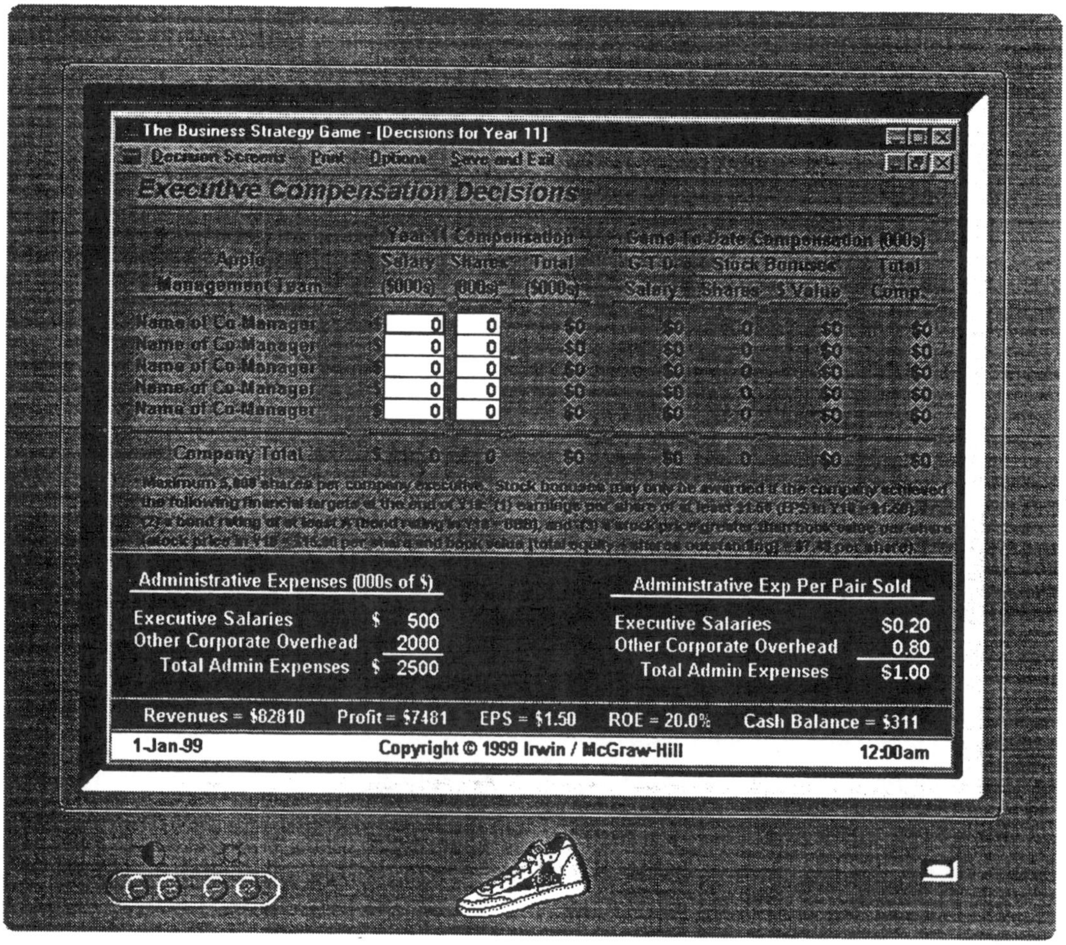

The absolute minimum for the combined salaries of all company co-managers is $500,000 per year, but the salaries paid to each manager should normally go up over time — more or less in line with the base wage increases granted to workers (unless, of course, the company is performing very poorly and economizing on management pay seems necessary).

Stock bonus awards, like salaries, can vary from co-manager to co-manager. All bonus awards must be in lots of 1,000 shares (that is, 1,000, 2000, 3,000, 4,000, or 5,000 shares) — your entries in the stock bonus data field are thus restricted to 0, 1, 2, 3, 4, or 5 since decision entries throughout the game are always in thousands. ***A maximum of 5,000 shares can be awarded to any one co-manager in any one year.***

Stock bonuses are awarded at management's discretion, provided the company's performance last year was good enough to warrant paying management bonuses. ***The company's board of directors has decreed that stock bonuses may be granted only if last year's ending stock price is above the book value per share, last year's earnings per share is at least $1.50 (the amount the company earned in Year 10), and the company's bond rating is A or higher.***[2] Anything short of these performance benchmarks indicates that shareholders have not, based on the company's prior year financial performance, benefited sufficiently from the actions and decisions you and your managers have made to justify awarding stock bonuses to managers. (The computer is programmed to block any entries for stock bonuses unless the minimum conditions set by the board are met.) Stock bonus awards will increase the number of shares of common stock outstanding but will ***not*** result in cash inflows from new stock sales since all shares issued to management are granted at no cost as part of the manager's compensation package.

> ***When activated by your instructor, the executive compensation screen allows you to pay higher salaries and award performance-based stock bonuses to the company's co-managers.***

The executive compensation option is intended to focus management attention on building shareholder wealth via a higher stock price and bigger earnings per share (while protecting the company's balance sheet and debt rating). Allowing for different salaries and stock bonuses for different co-managers also provides a strong incentive for each co-manager to fully participate in decisions, carry his or her share of the management load, and make a contribution to the company's performance that is recognized and appreciated by the other team members. As you can see from Exhibit 3-11, the computer will track the total compensation of each manager as the game progresses.

Don't be surprised if some portion of your grade on the simulation exercise is based on the total compensation (the last column on the executive compensation decision screen) that you have earned relative to other managers in both your company and other companies. Should this be the case, you and your co-managers will have to give careful consideration to several management compensation issues: (1) whether to boost managerial compensation through increased salaries (which is an additional expense to the company) or through stock bonuses (which may dilute earnings per share somewhat) and (2) how much in the form of additional salary and stock bonuses it will take to keep the compensation of your company's management team comparable to the compensation packages of managers in rival companies.

If and when the executive compensation screen comes into play, your instructor may provide further guidelines or requirements for management salary increases and stock bonus awards. You will need to observe these additional rules as well as those indicated above.

---

[2] *Book value per share equals total stockholders' equity divided by the total number of shares outstanding. A stock price below book value signals that the investment made by shareholders has diminished in value; a stock price above book value signals that investors believe the company's stock is worth more than the original amount invested. Thus, if your company's stock price is below book value per share, you have not enhanced shareholder value during your management tenure and should not, in the opinion of the board of directors, be awarded stock bonuses.*

THE DECISION MENU BAR

At the top of each decision screen (as well all other screens you will access when running *The Business Strategy Game*), is a menu bar. To move from one decision screen to another, use the mouse to click on the "Decision Screens" item in the menu bar. Then click on the desired decision screen option and the screen you have chosen will appear.

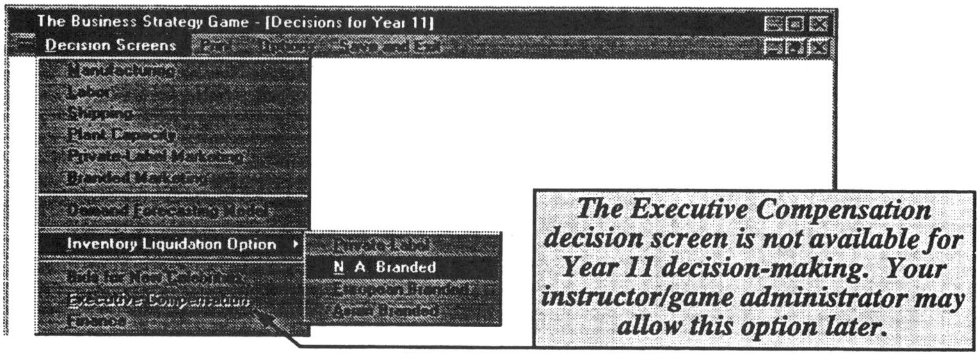

PRINTING YOUR DECISIONS. To print a hard-copy of the decisions you have entered, choose "Print" from the menu bar. Then choose "Print Decisions for Yx" and you will get a two-page decision printout. You may also choose "Printer Setup" to access the Windows printer setup dialog.

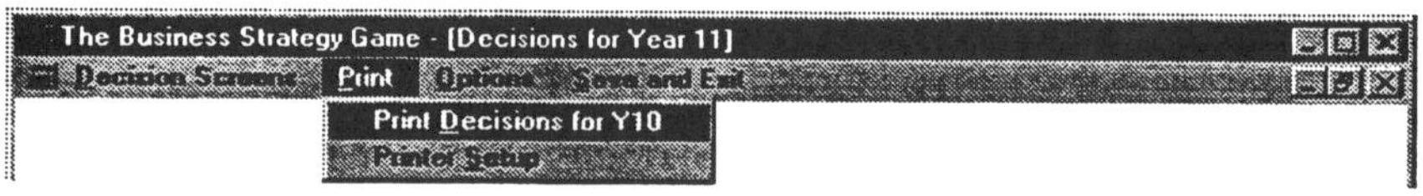

CALCULATION OPTIONS. *The Business Strategy Game* runs quite nicely on a computer with only a 66 MHz 486 DX2 processor and 8 MB of RAM. If you are using a machine that is slower or has less RAM and the response time on the recalculation for each new entry is too slow to suit you, you should try choosing "Options" and changing the "Calculation Mode" from "Automatic" to "Manual". When the calculation mode is set to automatic (the default setting), the program recalculates all of your company's projected data and reports (thousands of formulas) each time you press the [Enter] key after typing a new decision entry. On a fast computer the spreadsheet is automatically recalculated after every entry in the blink of an eye, but on a slower machine it could take several seconds. On a slow PC, when the calculation mode is set to manual, the company's projected data and reports are not recalculated until you tell the computer to do so by pressing the [F9] key or by choosing "Recalculate" from the menu bar.

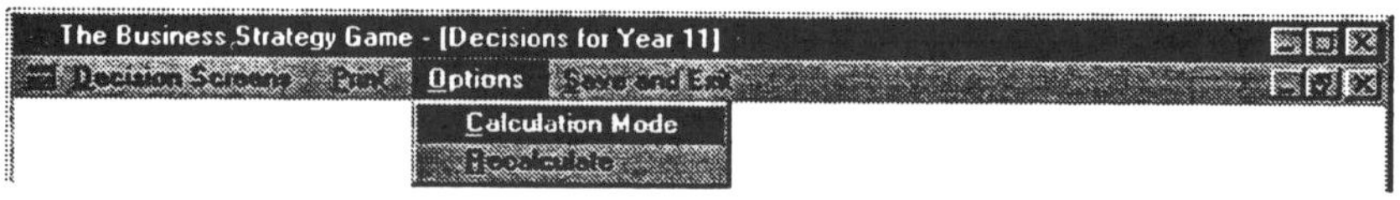

REMEMBER: *If you set the PC's calculation mode to manual, the performance projections at the bottom of each decision screen will not be accurate until* ***after*** *you press [F9] or choose Options/Recalculate from the menu bar.*

EXITING THE DECISION PROGRAM. ***When you are finished entering and printing your decisions, it is ABSOLUTELY ESSENTIAL that you choose "Save and Exit" from the decision menu bar.*** When you choose "Save Decisions and Return to Main Menu", the program saves the entries you have made onto your Company Data Disk. ***FAILURE TO EXIT PROPERLY FROM THE DECISION PROGRAM WILL RESULT IN LOST OR INCORRECT DECISION DATA.***

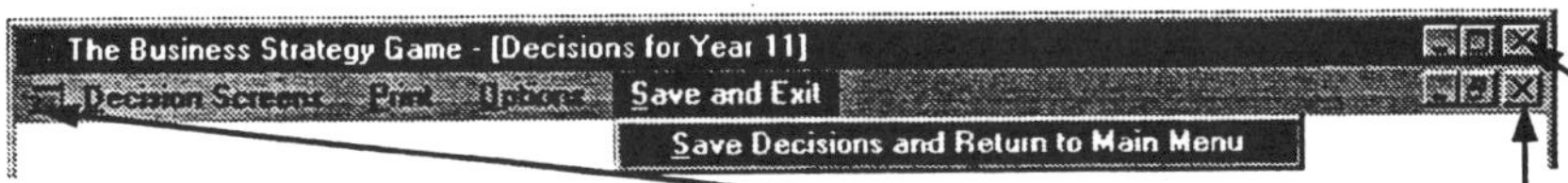

Do not use any of these buttons to close or exit the BSG program.

Do NOT terminate the program with the [X] in the top right corner of the Windows 95 (or Windows 98) screen. Furthermore, do NOT terminate the program Windows control-menu icon in the top left corner of the screen (the [–] for Windows 3.1 users). If you fail to use "Save and Exit", and instead, exit the program incorrectly, your data may not be saved and the program may be corrupted — you may have to re-install *The Business Strategy Game* company program files on your computer.

THE PROJECTIONS AT THE BOTTOM OF EACH SCREEN

On the bottom line of each decision screen are projections for sales revenues, after-tax profits, earnings per share of common stock outstanding (EPS), return on equity investment (ROE), and year-end cash balance. These five performance projections are a useful supplement to all the other decision support information provided on each screen and, like the other calculations, are automatically updated each time you make a decision entry or a what-if entry or revise the sales forecast. The calculations give you immediate feedback about how sensitive revenues, total after-tax profits, earnings per share, ROE, and the company's year-end cash balances are to particular decision entries and what-if entries. ***However, the revenue-profit-EPS-ROE-cash balance projections are not truly indicative of the company's performance for the year until you have entered a complete set of decisions, made a reasonable sales forecast, and entered what-if guestimates.*** Even then, the calculations provided are projections; actual outcomes are not known until the decisions of all companies are processed by the instructor/game administrator. How close the projections will be to the actual results depends heavily on the accuracy of your sales forecasts — inaccurate sales forecasts (either on the high side or the low side) will yield projections substantially different from the actual outcomes.

The projections at the bottom of each decision screen are not truly indicative of your company's performance until you have entered all decisions on all screens, including all sales forecasts and "what-if" estimates.

REACHING A FINAL SET OF DECISIONS

Once you and your co-managers have gone through all the decision screens and made a complete trial decision, used the demand forecast screen to project branded sales volume in each geographic market, entered sales forecasts, and entered what-if values, you and your co-managers can begin to rethink, refine, and perhaps seriously revise the initial entries — especially if you are not pleased with the performance projections for revenues, earnings, EPS, ROE, and year-end cash balance that appear at the bottom of each decision screen. Other strategies, decision options, and scenarios ought to be explored to see if the projected financial performance can be improved. This could entail adjusting your marketing effort up or down, revising manufacturing decisions to cut costs or modify inventories, altering shipping to reduce the adverse effects of exchange rate changes, raising or lowering sales forecast amounts, raising or lowering prices, using different financial options, and so on until you come up with a decision combination that holds ***realistic promise*** of producing attractive financial results. The calculations provided on each screen below the decision and what-if entries will prove invaluable in evaluating different decision combinations and strategic approaches. ***The demand forecasting screen is especially valuable for what-iffing different prices and marketing efforts in each geographic market to see what overall competitive effort it will take for your company to achieve the desired sales volume and market share.*** When you close in on a "final" set of decisions, it is worth taking a few minutes to review the detailed projections of company operations — you can obtain printouts of the ***projected outcomes*** for all eight management reports (just like those described and displayed in Section 2 of this manual) by selecting the sixth option on the Main Menu. When you are satisfied with all your decision entries, you are ready to exit the decision menu.

Section

4

SCORING, REPORTS, AND STRATEGIC PLANS

This section explains how company performance is scored, reviews the industry and company reports generated after each decision, and describes the important five-year strategic plan menu option. After you turn in the Company Data Disk with your decisions on it, the instructor/game administrator will process all the company decisions and return the disk to you with the year's financial results and actual competitive outcomes. On the disk you'll find three key industry reports — the Footwear Industry Report (which features a scoreboard of company performances and an array of industry and competitive information), the Benchmarking Report, and two competitor analysis reports. You'll also be able to review each of the eight company reports described in Section 2 and see what actually occurred for the year in all phases of company operations.

SCORING YOUR COMPANY'S PERFORMANCE

The Industry Scoreboard is the lead section in each year's issue of the Footwear Industry Report. The scoreboard section provides a rundown of each company's relative standing on revenues, after-tax earnings and earnings per share, return on equity investment, bond rating, stock price and company value, and strategy rating. These six performance measures, as a group, are the basis for judging your company's overall performance and determining your company's position in the industry rankings. If your company leads the industry in revenues from footwear sales, then your company will earn a score of 100 on the revenue component of performance. If your company is not the revenue leader, your company's score on the revenue component equals whatever percent your company's revenue is of the leader's revenue. For instance, if your company has revenues of $80 million versus $100 million for the industry's revenue leader, then your company's score on the revenue component of overall performance will be 80 (since your company's revenues are 80% of those of the company with the highest revenues).

Your company's performance scores on after-tax earnings (or EPS), return on equity, stock price (or stock value), and strategy rating are computed in similar fashion. If your company is the industry leader on any of these performance measures, your company's score is 100; otherwise your company's score equals whatever ***percentage*** of the industry leader's performance your company achieves. However, in the case of after-tax earnings (or EPS) and return on equity, it is possible that some companies will lose money and have a negative return on equity; the scores of money-losing companies for profits and ROE are set at zero. If all companies in the industry incur after-tax losses and/or have negative returns on equity investment, then all companies get scores of 0 on these two performance measures.

> ***Scoring in THE BUSINESS STRATEGY GAME is based on how your company performs relative to rival companies on six measures:***
>
> - ***Sales Revenues***
> - ***After-Tax Earnings or EPS***
> - ***Return On Equity***
> - ***Bond Rating***
> - ***Company Value or Stock Price***
> - ***Strategy Rating***

Each company's stock value is calculated by multiplying its latest stock price by the number of shares of common stock it has outstanding. The total dollar amount of all outstanding shares represents the value investors have placed on the company — the financial community refers to the total dollar value of all shares outstanding as "market capitalization." The company with the highest total stock value earns a perfect score on this performance measure. Every other company's score is calculated as a percentage of the leader's stock value. If your company's stock has a total market value of $120 million and the leader's is $150 million, then your company's score on the stock value performance measure will be 80 (because your company's value is 80% of the highest valued company). You should be aware that your instructor has the option of judging your company's performance solely on the basis of stock price rather than total stock value — you will be informed which measure is being used. Scoring is thus based on relative company performance rather than industry rank. ***The company with the best performance on each of the five measures (revenues, earnings, ROE, company value, and strategy rating) earns a perfect score of 100 on that measure; the scores of all other companies are calculated as a percent of the leader's performance.***

Performance scores on bond ratings are calculated a bit differently. An AAA rating (the highest) carries a score of 100 and a C bond rating (the lowest) carries a score of 0. The scores for the five ratings between AAA and C fall in-between the two extremes: an AA rating is scored as 90, an A rating equals 80, a BBB rating equals 60, a BB rating equals 40, and a B rating carries a score of 20.

HOW THE STRATEGY RATING IS CALCULATED. The strategy rating is designed to measure and rank the "power" of each company's strategy and the distinctiveness of the resulting market position. The intent is to reward companies that develop distinctive strategies to (1) stake out a particular position in the marketplace, (2) build a sustainable competitive advantage of one kind or another, and (3) develop a reputation with consumers as an industry leader on one or more product attributes or competitive factors. The higher a company's strategy rating, the more its strategy stands out in the industry.

> ***The Strategy Rating does not assess "how good" a company's strategy is; rather, it measures what a company is known for and how much a company stands apart from rivals.***

Table 4-1 describes the point system used in calculating strategy ratings. A listing of how many strategy rating points each company has earned on each power measure is at the bottom of page 8 of each year's Footwear Industry Report. Companies with the biggest number of strategy rating points on the power measures shown in Table 4-1 possess competitive advantage; companies with few strategy rating points suffer from competitive disadvantage.

Table 4-1: Strategy Rating Point System

Strategy Criterion	How Measured	Points Associated
Broad/Focused Product Line	To qualify as "broad or "focused", a company's weighted average number of models available in a branded region must be at least 15% **above** or **below** the region average.	1 point for each 5% that the company's weighted average number of models available in a branded region is above or below the region average (maximum of 15 points per region).
High Quality	To qualify as "high", a company's quality rating in a branded region must be at least 15 points **above** the region average.	1 point for each 5 points that the company's quality rating in a branded region exceeds the region average (maximum of 15 points per region).
Good Service	To qualify as "good", a company's service rating in a branded region must be at least 15 points **above** the region average.	1 point for each 5 points that the company's service rating in a branded region exceeds the region average (maximum of 15 points per region).
Brand Image	A company's brand image stands out when its image rating in a branded region is at least 15 points **above** the region average.	1 point for each 5 points that the company's image rating in a branded region exceeds the region average (maximum of 15 points per region).
Low Overall Cost	To qualify as "low cost", a company's operating costs per pair sold must be at least 10% **below** the average for branded regions or at least 3% **below** the private-label average.	1 point for each 3% that the company's operating cost per pair sold is below the average in a branded region or in the private-label segment.
Market Share Leadership	A company is designated a "market share leader" when its sales volume in a branded region or in the private-label segment is at least 15% **above** the region/segment average. The degree of leadership depends on how much the average is exceeded.	% Above Average — Points Assigned 15% - 25% — 4 points 25% - 25% — 6 points 35% - 50% — 9 points 50% - 100% — 13 points 100% - 200% — 18 points over 200% — 25 points
Superior Value	A company's product is considered to be of "superior value" when its value-price ratio in a branded region is at least 10% **above** the region average. The value-price ratio is calculated as follows: $\frac{(\text{Quality Rating} \times 2) + \text{Service Rating}}{\text{Price}}$	1 point for each 3% that the company's value-price ratio in a branded region exceeds the region average. No points are awarded in the private-label segment because price alone is the decisive competitive variable.
Global/Focused Coverage	To qualify for "global" market coverage, a company must derive at least 20% of its sales volume from **each** branded region. To qualify for "focused" market coverage, a company must derive at least 75% of its sales volume from a **single** branded region or from the private-label segment.	10 points for global coverage. –or– 10 points for focused coverage.

SPECIAL NOTE: *A company must sell at least 50,000 pairs in a particular geographic region to qualify for strategy rating points in that region.*

OVERALL COMPANY PERFORMANCE SCORES. Your company's overall performance score is a ***weighted average*** of the scores on the six individual performance measures — sales revenues, after-tax profits (or EPS), ROE, stock value (or stock price), bond rating, and strategy rating. The instructor or game administrator will announce the weights to be placed on each measure. The overall score your company receives relative to the scores of rival companies indicates how well your company is doing. For example, if the highest score of any company is 90 and your company's overall score is 60, then your company is doing two-thirds as well as the industry leader — which is not terrible but which leaves ample room for improvement. ***The highest possible overall score is 100.*** To obtain a score of 100, a company must be the best performing company on all six measures. An overall score in the 90s is excellent; an overall score in the 80s is very good. An overall score of 40 signals a need for serious strategy review and performance improvement.

GAME-TO-DATE PERFORMANCE. The Industry Scoreboard section shows not only the company standings for the immediately concluded year but also game-to-date company standings (all years combined, starting with Year 11). The game-to-date scores are based on ***cumulative*** revenues, ***cumulative*** after-tax profits, the overall game-to-date return on equity, current-year stock values, the latest bond rating, and the average strategy rating for the last three years (at the end of the game it is thus your company's three most recent strategy ratings that count in the overall standings, not the ratings that the company used to have early in the game).

The highest possible overall game-to-date score is 100; to obtain it, a company must be the industry leader on all six performance measures. As with current year scores, an overall game-to-date score in the 90s is excellent; a score in the 80s is very good. ***The two themes underlying the entire scoring procedure are that (1) standard yardsticks of business performance are utilized, and (2) each company's performance is judged relative to how well other companies in the industry have done.***

Judging company performance on a ***relative*** rather than an ***absolute*** basis is much sounder and fairer than rankings based on which company is in "first place" and which is in "last place" — a company that is in last place with an overall performance score of 70 is plainly doing much better than a company in last place with an overall score of 25. In an industry of ten companies, some company must rank tenth, but a tenth place company with a relative performance score of 70 is obviously a more solid performer than a tenth place company with a performance score of 25. Hence, it makes far more sense to base grading on a relative overall performance score than on absolute industry rankings.

You can see what the industry scoreboard looks like by reviewing the ***sample*** issue of the Footwear Industry Report in Appendix A at the end of the manual. Your instructor will determine the weights placed on each performance measure. Very likely, your instructor will rely heavily on your company's overall game-to-date performance score in determining the grade you and your co-managers receive on *The Business Strategy Game* exercise.

THE FOOTWEAR INDUSTRY REPORT

Following the Industry Scoreboard is a second section of the Footwear Industry Report containing industrywide information on total revenues and total pairs sold in each geographic market, year-end inventories, capacity utilization, materials prices, and a five-year demand forecast. Then there's a third section providing company-by-company details on the results of private-label bidding, prices charged, pairs sold, stockouts, quality and service ratings, numbers of retailers, advertising, brand image number of models in the product line, rebate programs, and assorted financial and operating statistics. The Footwear Industry Report concludes with a news bulletin announcing special developments, changes in costs or rates, and other matters of interest.

THE FIVE-YEAR DEMAND FORECAST. Each issue of the Footwear Industry Report contains projections of footwear demand for each of the next five years for private-label demand in North America, branded sales in the North America, branded sales in Europe, and branded sales in Asia (see the sample in Appendix A on page 90). The forecast is in terms of the total number of pairs that can be sold in each segment (to obtain the number of pairs which can be sold by each company ***on average***, divide the forecasted amounts by the number of companies in your industry). Be aware, though, that while the demand forecast is reliable in the sense of being based on the latest information and conditions available, it is not an absolute given. All demand forecasts in the Footwear Industry Report are subject to future changes in the S&P 500 Index and to unusually strong or weak efforts on the part of the industry to capture the potential demand. Thus, actual sales in any one particular year could in the extreme deviate from the forecast by as much as 10-15% should there be significant swings in the S&P 500 and industry efforts to capture the sales potentials prove unusually aggressive or unusually weak.

> ***Print and retain a copy of each year's Footwear Industry Report for your records. You may very well need to refer back to events that took place in previous years.***

The ***sample*** of the Footwear Industry Report contained on pages 90-100 of Appendix A shows the outcomes for a hypothetical industry. ***All figures in this sample are for illustrative purposes only*** but they do provide an indication about how sensitive footwear sales are to company differences in prices, quality, service, advertising, brand image, the number of retailers, the number of models offered, and rebate programs. Take a few minutes to familiarize yourself with the format and content of the sample in Appendix A.

The first issue of the Footwear Industry Report (FIR) will appear at the end of Year 11, so in making a decision for Year 11 you will not need to review the FIR (the screens will be blank). Except for Year 11, the first thing you should normally do when you get your Company Disk back with the year's happenings on it is to look at the FIR — ***always make a printout of the information it contains and retain it in your records***.

THE BENCHMARKING REPORT

The Benchmarking Report is a one-page statistical compilation showing how your company stacks up on materials costs, labor costs, reject rates, plant supervision costs, and manufacturing costs — see page 101 in Appendix A. As you can see, cost comparisons are provided for all Ohio plants, all Texas plants, all European plants, and all Asian plants and also for each market segment — private-label and branded (North America, Europe, and Asia). With this information, you can easily gauge your company's cost competitiveness and see exactly where your company has a cost advantage or disadvantage.

COMPETITOR ANALYSIS REPORTS

Two types of competitor analysis reports are available — one comparing the competitive efforts of each company in a given year and one that tracks the competitive effort of any company over time. The Competitor Strategy Comparisons Report shows how your company stacks up against rivals on each market share determinant in each of the four market segments — a sample is shown in Appendix A on page 102. How many branded pairs your company sells is a function of how your company's price compares against rivals' prices, how your company's product quality compares against rivals' quality, how your company's advertising effort compares against rivals' advertising, and so on. As you can see from reviewing the data in Appendix A, it is easy to compare one company's price, quality, model availability, service, advertising, retail network, image rating, and rebates against other companies and against the industry averages; these differences indicate who has how big a competitive advantage or disadvantage on each competitive measure, market-by-market. Such comparisons account for the sales and market share differences across companies and serve as a valuable guide in adjusting your competitive effort to obtain the targeted sales volume in the upcoming year.

The Company Tracking Report provides a year-by-year rundown on the prices, quality ratings, service ratings, advertising, rebates and so on for any rival company of interest (see the sample in Appendix A on page 103). This report highlights the competitive changes a company has made each year in each geographic market and will help you anticipate the moves they may make in the upcoming year. After 3 or 4 decision periods, you will find that some rivals are closer competitors than others. ***Printing out copies of the tracking report for these close competitors is the quickest and most accurate way to get a scouting report on key rivals*** — all the figures in this report come from information appearing in prior issues of the Footwear Industry Report. You can also print out a tracking report for your own company to review the competitive maneuvers that have been undertaken, see which were most successful in terms of pairs sold and market share, and help spot where improvements are needed.

Company Reports Containing Current-Year Results

When the Company Data Disk is returned, you'll be able to either view or obtain printouts of the eight company reports detailing the results of the company's operations for the past year. ***Ideally, you should print out a full set of reports*** — the manufacturing report, warehouse and sales report, marketing and administrative report, geographic profit report, cost report, income statement, year-end balance sheet, and cash flow report — ***for each co-manager***. See Section 2 of this manual for a description of the specific contents of these reports. ***Always retain at least one printout of the entire set of company reports in your records*** — you will ***not*** be able to go back later and obtain the results of earlier years since the results of each new decision are written over the results of prior years.

Looking Ahead: The Five-Year Strategic Plan

One of the most important menu selections on your Company Data Disk is the 5-Year Strategic Plan option. It allows you to build a five-year production plan for each plant, a five-year marketing plan for each market segment (private-label, North America, Europe, and Asia), and a five-year financial plan. There are seven entry screens, each with revenue-cost-profit projections and other calculations at the bottom to guide the tentative decisions and strategic course you chart. When you complete the plan, you can obtain a 3-page printout summarizing the outcomes and performance you can expect from the long-range strategy you've laid out. You'll find the 5-year planning option especially valuable in diagnosing weaknesses in your strategy, checking out the long-term consequences of particular actions (expanding a plant, issuing additional stock, taking on more debt, undertaking various automation options, and so on), and seeing whether your company's performance is likely to improve or worsen in the years ahead.

Don't be surprised if your instructor/game administrator asks you to prepare at least one 5-year strategic plan as the game progresses. While you may not welcome such an assignment, the fact is that ***making decisions one year at a time, with little or no view towards the future and few clues as to the longer-run consequences of current-year decisions, is no way to manage***. In practice, companies put considerable effort into trying to anticipate future market conditions, developing long-range strategies, and making 5-year financial projections because it enhances the quality of managerial decisions. For the same reason, you and your co-managers will find it worthwhile to go through the exercise of developing a five-year plan. Spending some quality time utilizing the 5-year strategic plan feature will give you good insights into how to improve your company's long-term competitive position and financial performance in the years ahead.

Section

5

USING THE COMPANY PROGRAMS AND DISKS

Your *Business Strategy Game* package consists of this manual and two 3½-inch floppy diskettes — the ***Company Program Disk*** and the ***Company Data Disk***. The Company Program Disk contains all of the Windows-executable programs necessary for running *The Business Strategy Game*. These programs must be installed to your computer's fixed disk drive, as described later in this section. All of your company's data and decisions are stored on the Company Data Disk. You will turn in your Company Data Disk to the game administrator at an agreed-upon time with your decision entries for the current year on it. When the game administrator returns your data disk, it will contain all the industry reports and your company's actual results for the year. You can then proceed with preparations for next year's decision. ***You are strongly urged to make backup copies of both disks before using them to start company operations.***

HARDWARE REQUIREMENTS

The Business Strategy Game is a Windows-based program. If you have access to a PC that operates with Windows 3.1 (or 3.11), Windows 95 (or 98), or Windows NT, you can successfully run the software. However, the computer set-up you use must have and meet all of the following capabilities and specifications:

- 6 MB of free file storage space on the fixed disk drive for installation of the files on the Company Program Disk.
- One high-density 3½-inch floppy disk drive.
- Printer access.

The Business Strategy Game runs quite nicely on a computer with only a 66 MHz 486 DX2 processor and 8 MB of RAM. If you use *The Business Strategy Game* on a machine with a slower processor or with less RAM, you may find the program a bit sluggish or even downright slow (as are most Windows programs when run on less powerful or older machines).

INSTALLING THE COMPANY PROGRAMS ON YOUR PC

If you are using a university computer lab, you can skip this section, (your instructor and/or the lab personnel will have already arranged for the necessary files to be installed). If you want to run *The Business Strategy Game* on your own PC, you will need a computer setup that meets or exceeds the specifications listed on the previous page.

WINDOWS 3.1 OR 3.11 USERS. The following instructions assume your computer's 3½-inch floppy disk drive is specified by the letter A. If your computer's 3½-inch floppy drive is specified as drive B, substitute the letter B for each instance that the instructions refer to drive A. To install the BSG Company Programs, follow this procedure:

Step 1: Insert your ***Company Program Disk*** into drive A.

Step 2: Choose **File** from the menu at the top of the Windows Program Manager screen and then choose **Run**.

Step 3: Type A:\INSTALL and press [Enter].

Step 4: Follow the installation instructions that appear on the screen.

WINDOWS 95, 98, OR NT USERS. The following instructions assume your computer's 3½-inch floppy disk drive is specified by the letter A. If your computer's 3½-inch floppy drive is specified as drive B, substitute the letter B for each instance that the instructions refer to drive A. To install the Company Program Disk, follow this procedure:

Step 1: Insert your ***Company Program Disk*** into drive A.

Step 2: Choose **Start** from the task bar at the bottom of the Windows screen and then choose **Run**.

Step 3: Type A:\INSTALL and press [Enter].

Step 4: Follow the installation instructions that appear on the screen.

When the installation procedure is complete, your Windows desktop will reappear on the screen and you will see a new window for *The Business Strategy Game* containing three new BSG shortcut icons. When you close this window (folder) the new BSG shortcuts will be transferred to the start menu, and the BSG folder will not reappear on your Windows desktop (unless you re-install the programs) — of course, you will always be able to access the BSG programs through the Start Menu. Before you close the BSG window, however, you may want to drag and drop the "BSG Company Operations" shortcut icon onto your Windows desktop. The BSG shortcut will then appear on your Windows desktop every time you turn on your PC (you can delete it any time you want).

OPERATING YOUR COMPANY

After completing the installation procedure, you are ready to operate your *Business Strategy Game* company for the first time. If you operate with Windows 95 (or 98) or NT, start the BSG program by clicking the **Start** button and then choose **Programs**, **The Business Strategy Game**, and **BSG Company Operations** (if you have a "BSG Company Operations" shortcut on your desktop, simply double-click the icon). If you operate with Windows 3.x, double-click on the "BSG Company Operations" icon in *The Business Strategy Game* window.

When you start the program, *The Business Strategy Game* title screen will appear first. After a few moments, the opening screen will appear followed by a welcome message. Carefully read any and all messages that are displayed. The program will ask you to insert your

Company Data Disk into the A drive. Unless otherwise directed by your instructor/game administrator, ***your Company Data Disk must ALWAYS be in the floppy drive when you run The Business Strategy Game.***

IDENTIFYING YOUR COMPANY

The first time you run *The Business Strategy Game,* a "New Company Identification" screen will appear (pictured below). You will be asked to supply the following information:

1. Your **Industry Number** (assigned to you by your instructor/game administrator)
2. Your **Company Letter** (assigned to you by your instructor/game administrator)
3. Your **Company Name** (must begin with your Company Letter; maximum 13 characters)
4. Your **Password** (choose a password beginning with any letter; maximum 13 characters)
5. The names and student ID numbers (or social security numbers) of each of the co-managers of your company's **Management Team.**

If you do not know your Industry Number or Company Letter (or if your instructor/game administrator has not yet assigned you an Industry Number or Company Letter), exit the Initial Setup routine immediately. If you enter the wrong Company Identification information, your instructor/game administrator can supply a special code word that allows you to correct your company identification entries.

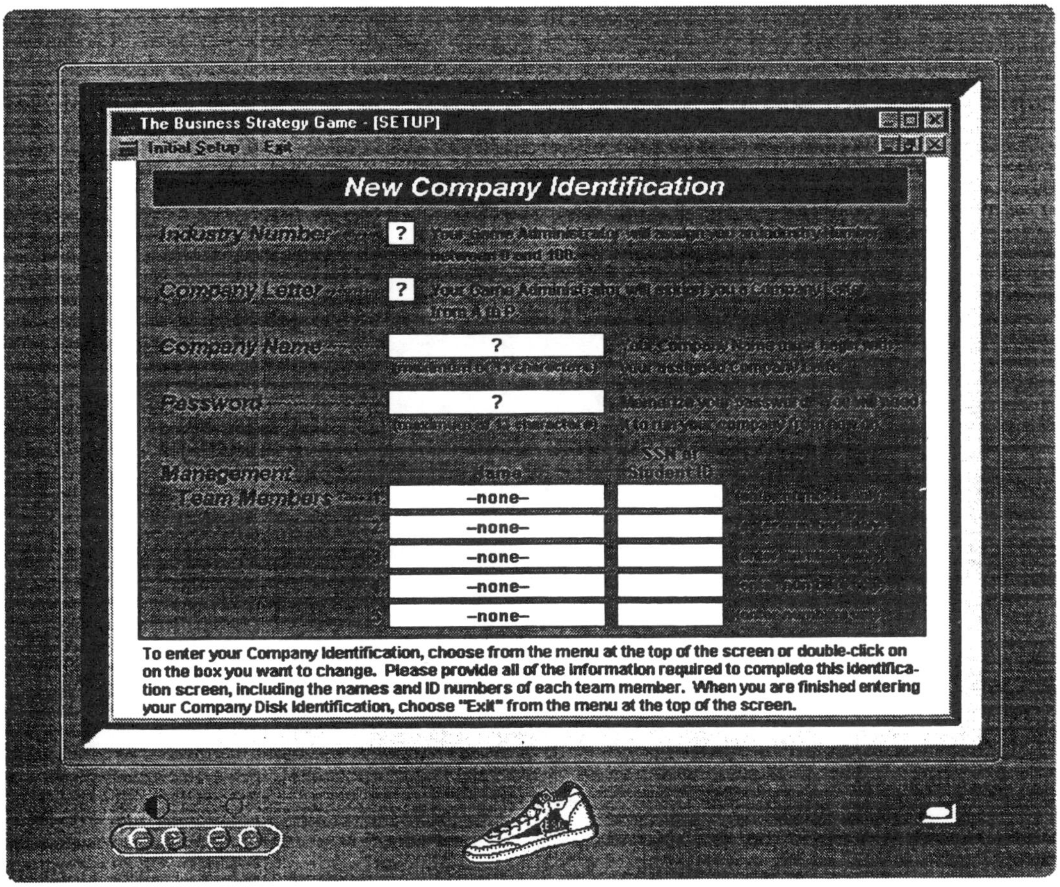

To enter your Industry Number, *double-click* on the white box beside "***Industry Number...***" label or else choose "Initial Setup" from the menu bar. Access each of the other entries in the same manner. Carefully follow all of the instructions that appear during the company identification sequence. ***When you are finished, choose "Exit" from the menu bar and your company identification entries will be automatically saved.***

> *Once you begin entering your company identification, you will not be allowed to exit until all of the required information (including at least one co-manager's name) has been entered.*

SPECIAL NOTE: Any time you want to exit a program or end your session with The Business Strategy Game, use the "Save and Exit" or "Exit" option provided in the menu bar at the top of each screen. Do not remove the Company Data Disk from the drive until you have exited completely from The Business Strategy Game using the "Exit" option provided on the Main Menu screen. FAILURE TO EXIT THE PROGRAM PROPERLY COULD RESULT IN THE LOSS OR CORRUPTION OF THE DATA ON YOUR COMPANY DATA DISK.

EXPLORING THE MAIN MENU

The Business Strategy Game Main Menu consists of eight items as shown below. You will use all of these menu items at one time or another during the course of company operations. Spend some time familiarizing yourself with the Main Menu.

You will use the first three selections on the Main Menu after each decision is processed; these three menu options allow you to view or obtain printouts of all the available reports (described earlier in this manual). You'll find the information in these reports essential in making decisions for the upcoming year. These reports are not available in making the decision for Year 11 because all companies had the same prices and competitive effort (models, quality, service, advertising, and so on) and the same operating results for Year 10, so copies of these reports going into Year 11 would add nothing about competitors or industry conditions beyond what has already been said. The fourth menu item allows you to view or print copies of the eight company reports described in Section 2; you will need to print a copy of this report for each co-manager after each decision is processed since it gives you the results of the prior year's operations. Whether you print a copy for use in making the Year 11 decision is optional since the information is the same as in the exhibits in Section 2.

DECISION ENTRIES FOR THE UPCOMING YEAR. The fifth item on the Main Menu is the one you will use to enter your decisions for the upcoming year. When you select it, the program will take a few moments to load the appropriate data and then the Decision Menu Bar will appear. The options on the Decision Menu Bar will take you to the decision screens for all the decisions you will need to make. Consult the discussions in Section 3 as needed for information about the "rules" and conditions surrounding these decisions.

PROJECTED COMPANY REPORTS FOR THE UPCOMING YEAR. As you arrive at a "final" or "near final" set of decisions, it is advisable to select the sixth item on the Main Menu to review your company's projected performance for the upcoming year. This option provides ***projections*** of the eight company reports based on the decision entries you have made for the upcoming year. Reviewing these projections carefully allows you to spot possible faulty decisions and to avoid doing something that produces an unwanted or preventable outcome. We recommend printing a copy of the projected company reports for later use in comparing how and why the actual results for the year in some cases deviated from the projected outcomes.

THE 5-YEAR STRATEGIC PLAN MENU OPTION. While you can "get by" with making only a decision for the upcoming year, it is very worthwhile to think ahead and develop a tentative strategy and set of decisions for 5 years at a time. This allows you to craft a proactive longer-range strategy and to manage the company for long-term strategic performance rather than worrying only about the upcoming year's performance and reacting to whatever happens. Making a 5-year strategic plan the first time will take a while longer, but after that it will be much simpler and quicker. Five-year plans are very helpful in exploring the long-term consequences of capacity expansion, automation options, alternative financing options, and the impact on next year's results of decisions made this year. ***Without doing some long-range thinking and crafting a 5-year plan, you'll find that your company's strategy will be more reactive than proactive — which can prove detrimental to your company's performance.***

> ***When you enter decisions in the 5-Year Strategic Plan program, you are NOT committing your company to the decisions in your plan — the entries are tentative and may be changed.***

If you develop a 5-year plan, you are not committing the company to the decisions you have entered for all 5 years. All decisions for the last 4 years of the plan can be changed after next year's decision is processed and you learn what actually happened. It is up to you and your co-managers to decide whether to "strategize" for only next year's decision or whether to build a more forward-looking decision plan that is updated annually. When you finish entering tentative decisions for 5 years, you can select a print option that provides a 5-year ***summary*** of performance projections for the company as a whole and for each geographic market. If you are dissatisfied with the performance projections, make changes (as needed) in the decision and what-if entries. It is wise to make a printout of your 5-year decision entries as well as the projected performance summary for easy reference.

Doing a 5-year plan is absolutely the best way to (1) understand the performance consequences of continuing the present strategy and (2) devise ways to improve the company's performance over the next several years. ***Making decisions one year at a time without looking further down the road is perilous.***

EXITING *THE BUSINESS STRATEGY GAME.* When you are ready to end your current session with *The Business Strategy Game*, select "Exit" from the menu bar at the top of the Main Menu screen. ***Always use the "Exit" option provided in the menu bar at the top of the Main Menu screen. Do not remove the Company Data Disk from the drive until you have exited completely from The Business Strategy Game using the "Exit" option provided on the Main Menu screen. Do not terminate the program with the Windows control icon [X] in the top right corner of the screen (or the [–] in the top left corner for Windows 3.x users). If you do, you may have to re-install The Business Strategy Game company program files on your computer. FAILURE TO EXIT THE PROGRAM PROPERLY COULD RESULT IN THE LOSS OR CORRUPTION OF THE DATA ON YOUR COMPANY DATA DISK.*** After a few seconds, the exit procedure will return you to Windows and you can remove your Company Data Disk.

RECOMMENDED DECISION MAKING PROCEDURES

In making decisions each year, we recommend that you and your co-managers go through the following steps:

Step 1: Make a printout of the FOOTWEAR INDUSTRY REPORT (you can skip this step in making the Year 11 decision since the first FIR issue appears with the Year 11 results). Having a hard copy of this report to consult as you make each new decision is virtually essential. ***Keep the printout*** so that you can refer back to the information later on if need be.

Step 2: Use the item 2 on the Main Menu to make a printout of the BENCHMARKING REPORT. (You should also skip this step for the first decision — the first issue of the Benchmarking Report will be available ***after*** the Year 11 results have been provided to you.)

Step 3: Beginning with the Year 12 decisions, use the third item on the Main Menu to make a printout of the COMPETITOR STRATEGY COMPARISONS for Year 11 (you will need at least one copy of this every year). You may also wish to print selected Company Tracking Reports (like the sample shown on page 103 in Appendix A) for any company of interest. The more you and your co-managers study the actions of key competitors and are able to anticipate their moves, the better you will be prepared to counter their strategies with offensive and defensive moves of your own.

Step 4: Use item 4 on the Main Menu to obtain a printout of your company's actual results for the past year and then review all eight COMPANY REPORTS line-by-line. ***It is perilous to rush into making decisions for the upcoming year without first having a good command of the prior year results and the strengths and weaknesses of your company's situation.*** See how your company compares on each of the items in the Benchmarking Report. Ideally, all company managers should have a copy of the company reports. You should keep one copy in your files in case you have to refer back to these results later on.

Step 5: After you have reviewed the Footwear Industry Report, the Benchmarking Report, the Competitor Analysis Reports, and the eight company reports, select the DECISION ENTRIES option (item 5 on the Main Menu). Make a complete trial decision by going through all the entries on the Manufacturing, Labor, Shipping, Plant, Private-Label Marketing, Branded Marketing, and Financial decision screens. Use the information in the industry and company reports and the on-screen calculations to guide your decisions for the upcoming year. Cycle through the various decision screens as many times as you wish — you will find that some cycling back and forth is essential.

> ***Special Note on Calculation Speed.*** *The Business Strategy Game runs quite nicely on a computer with only a 66 MHz 486 DX2 processor and 8 MB of RAM. If you are using a machine that is slower or has less RAM and the response time on the recalculation for each new entry is too slow to suit you, you should try choosing "Options" from the Decision Menu Bar and changing the "Calculation Mode" from "Automatic" to "Manual". When the calculation mode is set to automatic (the default setting), the program recalculates all of your company's projected data and reports (thousands of formulas) each time you press the [Enter] key after typing a new decision entry. On a fast computer this will happen in the blink of an eye, but on a slower machine it could take several seconds. When the calculation mode is set to manual, the company's projected data and reports are not recalculated until you tell the computer to do so by pressing the [F9] key or by choosing "Recalculate" from the menu bar. Remember that if you set the calculation mode to manual, the performance projections reported at the bottom of each decision screen will not be accurate until* ***after*** *you press [F9] or choose Options/Recalculate from the menu bar.*

Step 6: Make it a point to experiment with alternative actions and strategies — you can cycle back through the decision screens and make as many trial strategy options and decision combinations as you deem useful. The on-screen calculations and the demand forecasting screen make it easy to explore the effects of higher/lower selling prices, a stronger/weaker marketing effort, more/less production, different shipping combinations, different financial approaches, and alternative sales and what-if estimates. Fine tune your decision entries, what-if estimates, and sales estimates until you arrive at a course of action that holds promise in producing an attractive short-term and long-term outcome. We strongly urge that you ***make regular use the demand forecasting screen*** to determine what combination of prices and branded marketing effort it is likely to take to achieve the desired sales volume in each geographic market – learning to use this screen wisely is time well spent. It is a good idea to use the five-year strategic plan option to explore the effects of decisions over the following couple of years.

Step 7: As you near a final decision, choose "Save and Exit" from the menu bar at the top of any decision screen (every time you choose "Save Decision and Return to Main Menu", all of the decision entries you have made will be automatically saved to your Company Data Disk). When the Main Menu screen appears, select the sixth item to review your company's projected operating reports and financial statements for the upcoming year. It is an especially good idea to compare the information in the projected cost report against last year's actual cost report and the Benchmarking Report to see if any of the itemized cost projections are significantly different from last year. Check the geographic profit report against last year's geographic report to see if projected profits by area are higher or lower than last year. If needed, return to the Decision Entries selection on the Main Menu and make further adjustments in your decision plan if desired. Otherwise, print a copy of the PROJECTED COMPANY REPORTS for your records.

Step 8: When all of your decision entries and projected outcomes look satisfactory, return to the Decision Entries program and ***make two printouts of your final decision entries*** for the upcoming year using the "Print" option in the menu bar at the top of any decision entry screen. Turn in one copy with your Company Data Disk and keep the other for your records. ***Check the printout carefully to be sure, once again, that all your decision entries are as you want them.*** Then exit the Decision Entries program using "Save and Exit" from the menu bar at the top of any decision entry screen. ***When you choose "Save Decisions and Return to Main Menu", the program automatically saves all of your data and entries to your Company Data Disk.***

Step 9: If you have not already done so, choose Main Menu item 6 and print a complete set of your PROJECTED COMPANY REPORTS. Keep the copy of your Projected Company Reports and one copy of your Decision Entries printout for your records. ***Do not remove the Company Data Disk from the drive until you have exited completely from The Business Strategy Game using the "Exit" option provided in the menu bar at the top of the Main Menu screen. FAILURE TO EXIT THE PROGRAM PROPERLY COULD RESULT IN THE LOSS OR CORRUPTION OF THE DATA ON YOUR COMPANY DATA DISK.***

Step 10: Turn in your Company Data Disk containing your final decision along with a printout of your final decision to the game administrator by the agreed-upon time. The administrator will process the year's results and return your Company Data Disk, usually no later than the next day, with the actual company results and updated industry reports on it.

CONCLUDING COMMENTS

To do well in *The Business Strategy Game*, you and your co-managers will need to be shrewd analysts of the industry and competitive situation and you will need to manage internal operations efficiently. We urge that you make full use of the information in the Footwear Industry Report, the Benchmarking Report, the Competitor Analysis reports, and the company reports and become a conscientious student of what's happening inside and outside your company. You can't expect to do a first-rate job of managing your company if you don't know what's going on and aren't familiar with the information being provided. Appendix B contains a series of blank forms you may find helpful — one helps establish strategic and financial performance objectives, another can be used to do industry and competitive analysis, and one helps arrive at a company strategy. Good luck, and we hope you enjoy playing *The Business Strategy Game*.

Appendix A

SAMPLE INDUSTRY REPORTS

The following hypothetical Footwear Industry Report, Benchmarking Report, and Competitor Analysis reports provide a sample of the industry and competitive information you can get following each decision. The numbers in these samples should not be used as indicators of what might happen in the industry that you are competing in.

SAMPLE FOOTWEAR INDUSTRY REPORT

Year 15 Scoreboard

Rank	Company	Points	Trend*
1	Air Istotle	85	↑
2	Hyperlite	76	↓
3	Jaguar	76	↓
4	Excalibur	68	↑
5	Consultants	63	↑
6	Fortune Feet	60	↓
7	Inverness	58	↑
8	Glaca	53	↓
9	DynaBac	51	↓
10	BEST BUY	40	↓

Game-To-Date Scoreboard

Rank	Company	Points	Trend*
1	Hyperlite	87	↓
2	Jaguar	87	↓
3	Air Istotle	85	↔
4	Excalibur	70	↓
5	Fortune Feet	68	↑
6	Glaca	65	↓
7	Inverness	63	↑
8	DynaBac	62	↓
9	Consultants	61	↑
10	BEST BUY	48	↓

* Direction of change in score from prior year.

⇑ = most improved score over prior year.

Year 15 Scoring Breakdown

Company Name	Sales Revenues (5 point maximum) Revenues	Points	After-Tax Earnings (20 point maximum) Total Profit	EPS *	Points	Return On Equity (20 point maximum) ROE	Points
Air Istotle	$ 385,047	4	$ 120,225	$ 23.12	20	31.91%	17
BEST BUY	86,419	1	23,989	4.40	4	13.52	7
Consultants	420,803	5	83,880	10.82	9	21.76	12
DynaBac	149,874	2	33,791	6.76	6	14.57	8
Excalibur	194,254	2	54,495	11.90	10	37.64	20
Fortune Feet	305,516	4	51,511	10.73	9	19.90	11
Glaca	175,139	2	47,078	8.55	7	18.36	10
Hyperlite	435,597	5	68,982	16.42	14	27.81	15
Inverness	197,298	2	55,758	8.82	8	19.42	10
Jaguar	294,274	3	93,609	18.43	16	25.25	13
Industry Average	$ 264,422	3	$ 63,332	$ 12.00	10	23.02%	12

Company Name	Bond Rating (20 point maximum) Bond Rating	Points	Company Value (20 point maximum) All Shares*	Stock Price	Points	Strategy Rating (15 point maximum) Rating	Points
Air Istotle	AA	18	$ 1,711,996	$ 329¼	20	88	6
BEST BUY	AAA	20	531,648	97½	6	36	2
Consultants	AA	18	1,057,720	136½	12	100	7
DynaBac	AAA	20	743,250	148¾	9	86	6
Excalibur	AAA	20	915,634	200	11	72	5
Fortune Feet	AAA	20	927,744	193¼	11	68	5
Glaca	AAA	20	921,370	167½	11	50	3
Hyperlite	BBB	14	1,145,760	272¾	13	217	15
Inverness	AAA	20	839,170	132¾	10	113	8
Jaguar	AAA	20	1,731,467	340¾	20	63	4
Industry Average	AA	19	$ 1,052,576	$ 202	12	89	6

* Indicates the variable being used in the grading algorithm.

Game-To-Date Scoring Breakdown

	Sales Revenues (5 point maximum)		After-Tax Earnings (20 point maximum)			Return On Equity (20 point maximum)	
Company Name	Revenues	Points	Total Profit	EPS *	Points	ROE	Points
Air Istotle	$ 1,192,813	5	$ 360,462	$ 13.98	19	38.13%	17
BEST BUY	532,130	2	124,421	4.76	6	24.20	11
Consultants	1,121,856	4	226,700	6.69	9	25.39	11
DynaBac	798,536	3	205,922	8.24	11	28.57	13
Excalibur	820,031	3	236,029	9.78	13	39.50	18
Fortune Feet	1,083,914	4	220,486	9.42	13	32.06	14
Glaca	910,315	3	252,568	9.07	12	31.68	14
Hyperlite	1,316,625	5	314,881	14.96	20	44.51	20
Inverness	806,159	3	214,969	7.05	9	25.00	11
Jaguar	1,137,119	4	355,077	14.01	19	38.25	17
Industry Average	$ 971,950	4	$ 251,152	$ 9.79	13	32.73%	15

	Bond Rating (20 point maximum)		Company Value (20 point maximum)			Strategy Rating (15 point maximum)	
Company Name	Bond Rating	Points	All Shares*	Stock Price	Points	Rating	Points
Air Istotle	AA	18	$ 1,711,996	329¼	20	76	6
BEST BUY	AAA	20	531,648	97½	6	34	3
Consultants	AA	18	1,057,720	136½	12	87	7
DynaBac	AAA	20	743,250	148¾	9	85	6
Excalibur	AAA	20	915,634	200	11	72	5
Fortune Feet	AAA	20	927,744	193¼	11	82	6
Glaca	AAA	20	921,370	167½	11	69	5
Hyperlite	BBB	14	1,145,760	272¾	13	197	15
Inverness	AAA	20	839,170	132¾	10	134	10
Jaguar	AAA	20	1,731,467	340¾	20	86	7
Industry Average	AA	19	$ 1,052,576	202	12	92	7

* Indicates the variable being used in the grading algorithm.

Industry Overview

		Ohio	Texas	Europe	Asia	Overall
Global Production	Pairs Produced	4,329	18,103	16,698	45,936	85,066
	Pairs Rejected	102	734	786	2,519	4,141
	Capacity Utilization	72.2%	100.6%	98.2%	106.8%	101.3%
	Long-Wear Materials	1.7%	35.3%	61.3%	36.9%	39.6%
		P–Label	N.A.	Europe	Asia	Overall
Global Sales	Pairs Available	28,748	35,355	25,354	19,735	109,192
	Pairs Sold	9,500	20,768	14,376	14,239	58,883
	Pairs Liquidated	0	1,846	0	0	1,846
	Ending Inventory	19,248	12,741	10,978	5,496	48,463

Demand Forecast (000s of pairs)

	Private-Label	Branded Markets N.A.	Europe	Asia	World Total
Year 16	9,600	22,844	19,052	19,325	70,821
Year 17	9,400	21,930	22,100	24,349	77,780
Year 18	10,150	22,588	25,194	29,219	87,151
Year 19	11,050	23,491	28,218	33,310	96,069
Year 20	11,400	21,142	31,039	36,308	99,889

Year 15 Materials Prices

	Normal-Wear	Long-Wear
Base Price	$6.00	$12.00
Adjustment for:		
Cap. Utilization	0.08	0.15
Materials Mix	-0.44	0.87
Market Price	$5.64	$13.03

Plant Capacity

Company	Plant Capacity On-Line in Year 15: Ohio	Texas	Europe	Asia	Planned Changes for Year 16: Texas	Europe	Asia	Year 16 Capacity
A	1,000	2,000	3,000	10,000	0	0	0	16,000
B	1,000	2,000	0	1,000	0	0	0	4,000
C	0	0	6,000	8,000	0	0	0	14,000
D	1,000	2,000	0	2,000	0	0	0	5,000
E	0	3,000	0	0	0	1,000	0	4,000
F	0	0	5,000	4,000	0	0	0	9,000
G	1,000	2,000	0	3,000	0	0	2,000	8,000
H	0	3,000	3,000	3,000	0	0	0	9,000
I	1,000	2,000	0	3,000	0	0	0	6,000
J	1,000	2,000	0	9,000	0	0	0	12,000
Total	6,000	18,000	17,000	43,000	0	1,000	2,000	87,000

The Private-Label Market

Co.	Model Availability	Quality Rating	Bid Price	Warehouse Operations (000s of pairs) Available	Offered	Sold	Inventory	Market Share %
A	89	89	$33.99	5,636	5,700	0	5,636	0.0
B	100	102	42.50	1,121	1,599	0	0	0.0
C	150	106	31.99	5,200	5,200	0	5,200	0.0
D	50	53	47.00	1,288	1,250	0	1,288	0.0
E	0	0	0.00	0	0	0	0	0.0
F	177	128	26.90	3,834	3,800	2,700	1,134	28.4
G	0	0	0.00	0	0	0	0	0.0
H	50	94	21.97	6,840	6,900	6,800	40	71.6
I	0	0	0.00	0	0	0	0	0.0
J	92	84	28.97	5,950	5,950	0	5,950	0.0
Overall	118	109	$38.89	29,869	30,399	9,500	19,248	16.7

The Branded Markets

Co.	Model Availability N.A.	Europe	Asia	Quality Ratings N.A.	Europe	Asia
A	148	150	150	127	120	123
B	100	100	61	101	115	125
C	164	174	176	101	100	99
D	50	59	56	210	219	216
E	250	250	250	174	169	179
F	250	250	158	152	153	117
G	52	250	250	161	134	129
H	250	250	250	228	227	224
I	50	50	50	202	198	199
J	141	148	143	116	117	116
Average	145	170	154	161	159	153

The Branded Markets
(continued)

Co.	Service Ratings N.A.	Service Ratings Europe	Service Ratings Asia	Number of Retail Outlets N.A.	Number of Retail Outlets Europe	Number of Retail Outlets Asia
A	187	203	209	4,000	1,000	500
B	100	100	130	4,000	1,000	650
C	165	165	165	10,000	3,000	4,000
D	168	180	180	3,300	1,200	1,200
E	235	218	126	1,200	450	180
F	165	235	235	4,000	1,200	1,200
G	165	129	191	1,500	1,500	1,300
H	247	250	250	1,500	500	500
I	168	168	203	2,000	1,000	1,000
J	183	159	194	3,500	2,000	2,000
Average	177	178	188	3,444	1,317	1,253

Co.	Year 15 Advertising ($000s) N.A.	Year 15 Advertising ($000s) Europe	Year 15 Advertising ($000s) Asia	Image Rating N.A.	Image Rating Europe	Image Rating Asia
A	4,250	2,500	2,250	58	54	66
B	3,500	1,500	1,500	58	46	62
C	5,000	3,500	3,000	58	62	70
D	5,800	4,500	4,500	62	66	74
E	4,000	2,700	500	121	122	72
F	4,500	2,500	2,000	96	99	102
G	4,000	2,500	2,600	103	111	130
H	5,500	3,000	3,000	214	206	250
I	5,750	4,500	4,000	140	156	175
J	5,000	3,500	3,500	62	54	62
Average	4,783	3,133	2,685	102	102	106

The Branded Markets
(continued)

Co.	Customer Rebates N.A.	Customer Rebates Europe	Customer Rebates Asia	Selling Prices N.A.	Selling Prices Europe	Selling Prices Asia
A	$5	$5	$5	$43.99	$43.99	$41.99
B	4	3	4	55.00	52.50	51.99
C	3	3	3	34.99	34.99	33.99
D	5	5	5	65.00	64.00	60.00
E	10	10	7	72.56	73.77	71.99
F	5	5	5	65.00	65.00	40.00
G	3	4	4	53.99	56.49	51.99
H	0	0	0	62.99	62.49	56.75
I	4	4	4	58.99	57.99	55.99
J	2	2	2	45.00	47.00	37.50
Average	$4.0	$4.0	$3.9	$57.06*	$57.14*	$50.22*

Co.	Pairs Sold N.A.	Pairs Sold Europe	Pairs Sold Asia	Sales Gained (Lost) Because of Stockouts N.A.	Sales Gained (Lost) Because of Stockouts Europe	Sales Gained (Lost) Because of Stockouts Asia
A	3,870	2,722	2,264	0	0	237
B	677	511	430	0	0	46
C	5,445	3,558	2,981	0	0	313
D	938	731	702	0	0	74
E	1,368	830	469	0	0	40
F	1,158	918	1,624	0	0	(1,094)
G	1,081	1,018	1,140	0	0	120
H	1,988	1,311	1,393	0	0	146
I	1,357	1,095	960	0	0	101
J	2,886	1,682	2,276	0	0	18
Total	20,768	14,376	14,239	0	0	1

* Region averages do not include the prices of companies selling fewer than 100,000 pairs (since such companies are not significant competitors in the region).

Celebrity Endorsements

Celebrity	Consumer Appeal Index	Contract Status: Contract Holder (year signed)	Contract Status: Terms ($000/yr.)	Standard Contract Period	Year Next Available For Bid
José Montana	50	Air Istotle (Y15)	$2001	2 years	Year 17
Oprah Letterman	100	Hyperlite (Y14)	$4511	3 years	Year 17
Angelica Freestyle	70	Hyperlite (Y11)	$1000	5 years	Year 16
Tiger Greene	90	Hyperlite (Y14)	$4011	2 years	Year 16
Freon Deon	50	Consultants (Y15)	$2950	3 years	Year 18
Karioki Footsu	100	Inverness (Y12)	$2500	4 years	Year 16
Sir Charles Dunkem	40	Air Istotle (Y15)	$2360	1 years	Year 16
Sally Strideright	55	Hyperlite (Y13)	$1359	3 years	Year 16
Monica Sellars	75	Glaca (Y13)	$2051	4 years	Year 17
Jacques LaFeet	30	[unsigned]	$0	2 years	Year 16
Pélé Payless	60	Excalibur (Y14)	$2699	3 years	Year 17
Mikee Nikee	80	Hyperlite (Y14)	$4011	4 years	Year 18

Year 15 Strategy Rating Comparisons

Measure of Strategic Performance		Strategy Rating Points by Company: A	B	C	D	E	F	G	H	I	J
Product Line (broad/focused)	N.A.	·	6	·	13	14	14	13	14	13	·
	Europe	·	8	·	13	10	10	10	10	14	·
	Asia	·	12	·	13	12	·	12	12	14	·
High Quality	N.A.	·	·	·	11	3	·	·	14	9	·
	Europe	·	·	·	13	·	·	·	14	9	·
	Asia	·	·	·	13	5	·	·	14	9	·
Good Service	N.A.	·	·	·	·	11	·	·	14	·	·
	Europe	4	·	·	·	7	11	·	14	·	·
	Asia	4	·	·	·	·	9	·	12	·	·
Brand Image	N.A.	·	·	·	·	5	·	·	15	9	·
	Europe	·	·	·	·	5	·	·	15	12	·
	Asia	·	·	·	·	·	·	5	15	14	·
Overall Low Cost	P-Label	·	·	·	·	·	·	·	5	·	·
	N.A.	9	·	8	·	·	·	·	·	·	10
	Europe	6	·	8	·	·	·	·	·	·	5
	Asia	7	·	8	·	·	·	·	·	·	8
Market Share Leadership	P-Label	·	·	·	·	·	18	·	25	·	·
	N.A.	13	·	18	·	·	·	·	·	·	9
	Europe	13	·	18	·	·	·	·	·	·	4
	Asia	13	·	18	·	·	·	·	·	·	13
Superior Value	N.A.	4	·	6	·	·	·	·	8	·	·
	Europe	5	·	6	·	·	·	·	9	·	·
	Asia	·	·	·	·	·	6	·	7	·	4
Market Coverage	Global	10	10	10	10	·	·	10	·	10	10
	Focused	·	·	·	·	·	·	·	·	·	·
Total Strategy Rating Points		88	36	100	86	72	68	50	217	113	63

Compensation and Productivity

Co.	Annual Wages ($000s per worker) Ohio	Texas	Europe	Asia	Total Compensation ($000s per worker) Ohio	Texas	Europe	Asia
A	$16.0	$14.0	$11.0	$4.5	$23.8	$20.6	$15.1	$7.4
B	16.8	13.1	0.0	3.5	21.2	20.6	0.0	4.8
C	0.0	0.0	11.0	4.0	0.0	0.0	15.7	6.0
D	18.5	14.6	0.0	4.2	27.9	20.3	0.0	6.5
E	0.0	13.3	0.0	0.0	0.0	21.6	0.0	0.0
F	0.0	0.0	12.0	4.0	0.0	0.0	20.6	9.1
G	0.0	13.3	0.0	4.2	0.0	19.6	0.0	8.7
H	0.0	13.7	11.1	6.1	0.0	24.5	19.1	10.6
I	0.0	13.1	0.0	2.8	0.0	28.9	0.0	3.7
J	16.6	13.3	0.0	4.0	22.0	20.9	0.0	6.1
Average	$17.0	$13.5	$11.3	$4.1	$23.7	$22.1	$17.6	$7.0

Co.	Incentive Pay (as % of total compensation) Ohio	Texas	Europe	Asia	Worker Productivity (pairs per worker per year) Ohio	Texas	Europe	Asia
A	32.8	32.0	27.0	39.4	4,730	3,772	2,712	3,659
B	20.7	36.3	0.0	27.6	2,431	4,262	0	2,667
C	0.0	0.0	29.9	33.2	0	0	3,232	3,059
D	33.7	28.0	0.0	35.4	6,262	3,251	0	3,063
E	0.0	38.6	0.0	0.0	0	3,711	0	0
F	0.0	0.0	41.7	56.4	0	0	3,807	4,501
G	0.0	32.1	0.0	52.0	0	3,369	0	4,458
H	0.0	44.2	42.0	42.5	0	5,162	3,605	4,516
I	0.0	54.6	0.0	23.5	0	5,730	0	2,865
J	24.6	36.3	0.0	34.3	4,521	4,466	0	3,211
Average	27.9	37.8	35.1	38.3	4,486	4,215	3,339	3,555

Comparative Financials

Co.	Income Statement Data ($000s): Manufacturing Cost	Warehouse Expense	Marketing Expense	Administrative Expense	Operating Profit	Interest Expense	Extraordinary Gain(Loss)	Miscellaneous Data: Common Stock (shares)	Dividends ($/share)	Net Profit ($/pair)
A	141,975	24,082	32,962	11,012	175,016	3,266	0	5,200	2.50	13.58
B	29,554	10,256	9,604	3,650	33,355	-915	0	5,450	0.70	14.83
C	207,524	27,145	30,407	10,508	139,775	13,797	-6,150	7,750	0.80	7.00
D	64,201	9,611	23,485	4,572	48,004	-270	0	5,000	0.60	14.25
E	70,294	13,790	29,913	2,501	77,756	-95	0	4,580	4.50	20.43
F	134,762	16,340	21,769	9,000	83,418	9,830	0	4,800	1.35	8.05
G	69,365	17,735	17,211	5,150	65,677	-1,577	0	5,504	1.00	14.53
H	236,564	31,999	38,003	9,000	120,031	21,484	0	4,200	0.00	6.00
I	76,221	13,289	23,167	6,050	78,571	-1,083	0	6,320	0.70	16.34
J	106,555	24,011	19,957	10,504	133,248	-480	0	5,080	1.30	13.68
Avg.	113,702	18,826	24,648	7,195	95,485	4,396	-615	5,388	1.34	12.87

Co.	Balance Sheet Data ($000s): Ending Cash Balance	Total Assets	Short-Term Debt	Bonded Debt	Total Liabilities	Accum. Retained Earnings	Stockholders' Equity	Financial Ratios: Days of Inventory	Times Interest Earned	Debt to Assets Ratio
A	0	645,526	108,696	126,000	268,773	312,886	376,753	515	53.59	0.36
B	17,874	194,023	0	9,600	16,620	128,049	177,403	1,104	n.m.*	0.05
C	0	554,120	11,911	128,500	168,694	221,521	385,426	216	10.13	0.25
D	81,640	258,011	0	19,600	26,057	210,954	231,954	459	n.m.*	0.08
E	37,576	168,944	0	15,900	24,150	140,214	144,794	185	n.m.*	0.09
F	0	321,188	15,695	26,820	62,360	213,203	258,828	207	8.49	0.13
G	81,636	278,708	0	6,000	22,340	250,135	256,368	332	n.m.*	0.02
H	0	446,753	79,529	98,200	198,740	214,539	248,013	140	5.59	0.40
I	94,701	306,525	0	9,900	19,469	212,595	287,056	283	n.m.*	0.03
J	0	453,437	47,889	7,600	82,716	345,387	370,721	418	n.m.*	0.12
Avg.	31,343	362,724	26,372	44,812	88,992	224,948	273,732	117	21.72	0.20

* Not meaningful. Times-interest-earned = operating profit / interest expense. If either operating profit or interest expense is negative, the calculation is deemed not meaningful.

Key Financial and Cost Values

Exchange Rates	Japanese Yen / $	118.00
	Eurodollars / $	1.6600
Interest Rates	AAA Bonds	7.50%
	S-T Prime	7.50%
Base Materials Prices (base $ per pair)	Normal-Wear	7.50
	Long-Wear	12.50
Private-Label Specs	Minimum Models	50
	Minimum Quality	50
Shipping Costs ($ per pair)	Within a Region	0.25
	Between Regions	0.50
Private-Label Conversion Cost ($/pair)		0.50

Import Tariffs ($ per pair)	N.A. to Europe	4.00
	N.A. to Asia	8.00
	Europe to N.A.	0.00
	Europe to Asia	8.00
	Asia to N.A.	0.00
	Asia to Europe	4.00
Cost of Faster Delivery ($ per pair)	3-weeks	0.25
	2-weeks	0.75
	1-week	1.50
Base Plant Supervision Cost ($/worker)		6,000
Retailer Support Cost ($/retail outlet)		100
Cost of Bid for Celebrities ($000s)		100

Headline News

Effective Year 16, the prime rate on short-term loans will be 7.5% and the AAA bond interest rate will be 7.5%.

Materials suppliers today announced the introduction of new shoe fabrics and a narrower price differential between normal-wear and long-wear materials. Initially, both normal and long-wear materials prices will increase to allow fast recovery of the R&D costs associated with bringing the new fabrics to market. Effective Year 16, the base price of normal-wear materials will be $7.50 per pair and the base price of long-wear materials will be $12.50 per pair.

The S&P for year 15 was 1118.67
The S&P for year 16 will be 1133.85

SAMPLE BENCHMARKING REPORT

Plant Benchmarks		Ohio	Texas	Europe	Asia
Reject Rates	High	3.60%	6.00%	6.20%	6.80%
	Low	1.00	0.50	2.20	0.50
	Average	2.23	3.41	4.35	4.11
Average Production Methods Improvements (per pair of capacity)	High	$ 0.38	$ 0.46	$ 0.25	$ 0.32
	Low	0.10	0.05	0.05	0.03
	Average	0.21	0.24	0.16	0.15
Materials Cost (per pair produced)	High	$ 6.17	$ 12.07	$ 12.60	$ 12.29
	Low	5.37	5.37	7.80	5.37
	Average	5.66	8.58	10.09	8.73
Labor Cost (per pair produced)	High	$ 9.26	$ 6.31	$ 5.86	$ 2.52
	Low	4.94	4.93	5.03	1.31
	Average	6.19	5.55	5.56	2.02
Plant Supervision Cost (per worker)	High	$ 5,763	$ 5,911	$ 5,910	$ 6,000
	Low	5,401	5,278	4,320	4,185
	Average	5,626	5,606	5,347	5,125
Manufacturing Cost (per pair produced)	High	$ 25.20	$ 37.48	$ 31.42	$ 29.12
	Low	15.39	14.81	19.47	12.26
	Average	18.18	22.04	24.55	17.84

Market Segment Benchmarks		P-Label	N.A.	Europe	Asia
Manufacturing Cost (per pair sold)	High	$ 18.97	$ 31.68	$ 32.27	$ 30.25
	Low	13.45	15.39	15.70	14.74
	Average	16.21	23.05	22.10	20.22
Warehouse Expenses (per pair sold)	High	$ 2.25	$ 4.16	$ 12.22	$ 10.27
	Low	1.62	2.21	2.06	1.36
	Average	1.93	2.71	6.18	3.69
Marketing Expenses (per pair sold)	High	$ 0.00	$ 12.29	$ 12.45	$ 10.45
	Low	0.00	2.76	2.64	2.01
	Average	0.00	6.87	6.29	5.27
Administrative Expenses (per pair sold)	High	$ 1.41	$ 2.26	$ 2.26	$ 2.26
	Low	0.78	0.78	0.78	0.78
	Average	1.09	1.43	1.43	1.43
Operating Profit (per pair sold)	High	$ NA	$ 30.70	$ 27.86	$ 28.43
	Low	NA	11.96	10.30	9.18
	Average	NA	21.05	19.83	19.60

NA — Manufacturing cost per pair produced data not available if less than four plants operating in the region.
Operating profit per pair sold data not available if less than four companies competing in the region.

SAMPLE COMPETITOR ANALYSIS REPORTS

Industry 5 | **Competitor Strategy Comparisons** | **Year 15**

Competitive Measure	A	B	C	D	E	F	G	H	I	J	K	L	M	N	O	P	Avg.
	Company																
Private-Label Market																	
Model Availability	89	100	150	50	0	177	0	50	0	92	.	.	.	.	.	.	101
Quality Rating	89	102	106	53	0	128	0	94	0	84	.	.	.	.	.	.	94
Bid Price	33.99	42.50	31.99	47.00	0.00	26.90	0.00	21.97	0.00	28.97	.	.	.	.	.	.	33.33
Pairs Offered	5,636	1,121	5,200	1,250	0	3,800	0	6,840	0	5,950	.	.	.	.	.	.	4,257
Pairs Sold	0	0	0	0	0	2,700	0	6,800	0	0	.	.	.	.	.	.	1,357
Market Share (%)	0.0	0.0	0.0	0.0	0.0	28.4	0.0	71.6	0.0	0.0	.	.	.	.	.	.	14.3
N.A. Branded Market																	
Model Availability	148	100	164	50	250	250	52	250	50	141	.	.	.	.	.	.	146
Quality Rating	127	101	101	210	174	152	161	228	202	116	.	.	.	.	.	.	157
Service Rating	187	100	165	168	235	165	165	247	168	183	.	.	.	.	.	.	178
Number of Retailers	4,000	4,000	10,000	3,300	1,200	4,000	1,500	1,500	2,000	3,500	.	.	.	.	.	.	3,500
Advertising Budget	4,250	3,500	5,000	5,800	4,000	4,500	4,000	5,500	5,750	5,000	.	.	.	.	.	.	4,730
Image Rating	58	58	58	62	121	96	103	214	140	62	.	.	.	.	.	.	97
Customer Rebates	5	4	3	5	10	5	3	0	4	2	.	.	.	.	.	.	4
Selling Price	43.99	55.00	34.99	65.00	72.56	65.00	53.99	62.99	58.99	45.00	.	.	.	.	.	.	55.75
Pairs Demanded [1]	3,870	677	5,445	938	1,368	1,158	1,081	1,988	1,357	2,886	.	.	.	.	.	.	2,077
Pairs Sold	3,870	677	5,445	938	1,368	1,158	1,081	1,988	1,357	2,886	.	.	.	.	.	.	2,077
Market Share (%)	18.6	3.3	26.2	4.5	6.6	5.6	5.2	9.5	6.5	13.9	.	.	.	.	.	.	10.0
European Branded Market																	
Model Availability	150	100	174	59	250	250	250	250	50	148	.	.	.	.	.	.	168
Quality Rating	120	115	100	219	169	153	134	227	198	117	.	.	.	.	.	.	155
Service Rating	203	100	165	180	218	235	129	250	168	159	.	.	.	.	.	.	181
Number of Retailers	1,000	1,000	3,000	1,200	450	1,200	1,500	500	1,000	2,000	.	.	.	.	.	.	1,285
Advertising Budget	2,500	1,500	3,500	4,500	2,700	2,500	2,500	3,000	4,500	3,500	.	.	.	.	.	.	3,070
Image Rating	54	46	62	66	122	99	111	206	156	54	.	.	.	.	.	.	98
Customer Rebates	5	3	3	5	10	5	4	0	4	2	.	.	.	.	.	.	4
Selling Price	43.99	52.50	34.99	64.00	73.77	65.00	56.49	62.49	57.99	47.00	.	.	.	.	.	.	55.82
Pairs Demanded [1]	2,722	511	3,558	731	830	918	1,018	1,311	1,095	1,682	.	.	.	.	.	.	1,438
Pairs Sold	2,722	511	3,558	731	830	918	1,018	1,311	1,095	1,682	.	.	.	.	.	.	1,438
Market Share (%)	18.9	3.6	24.7	5.1	5.8	6.4	7.1	9.1	7.6	11.7	.	.	.	.	.	.	10.0
Asian Branded Market																	
Model Availability	150	61	176	56	250	158	250	250	50	143	.	.	.	.	.	.	154
Quality Rating	123	125	99	216	179	117	129	224	199	116	.	.	.	.	.	.	153
Service Rating	209	130	165	180	126	235	191	250	203	194	.	.	.	.	.	.	188
Number of Retailers	500	650	4,000	1,200	180	1,200	1,300	500	1,000	2,000	.	.	.	.	.	.	1,253
Advertising Budget	2,250	1,500	3,000	4,500	500	2,000	2,600	3,000	4,000	3,500	.	.	.	.	.	.	2,685
Image Rating	66	62	70	74	72	102	130	250	175	62	.	.	.	.	.	.	106
Customer Rebates	5	4	3	5	7	5	4	0	4	2	.	.	.	.	.	.	4
Selling Price	41.99	51.99	33.99	60.00	71.99	40.00	51.99	56.75	55.99	37.50	.	.	.	.	.	.	50.22
Pairs Demanded [1]	2,027	384	2,668	628	429	2,718	1,020	1,247	859	2,258	.	.	.	.	.	.	1,424
Pairs Sold	2,264	430	2,981	702	469	1,624	1,140	1,393	960	2,276	.	.	.	.	.	.	1,424
Market Share (%)	15.9	3.0	20.9	4.9	3.3	11.4	8.0	9.7	6.7	16.0	.	.	.	.	.	.	10.0

[1] Pairs Demanded = Pairs Sold + Stockouts – Sales Gained from Stockouts. This is the truest measure of the demand generated by a company's competitive strategy, since stockouts represent unsatisfied demand and sales gains from stockouts are a windfall resulting from the demand misjudgements of rivals.

Note: Companies with sales of fewer than 100,000 pairs are not included in industry averages, except for pairs demanded, pairs sold, and market share.

Industry 5 — **Competitor Tracking Report** — Company A

Competitive Measure	Y10	Y11	Y12	Y13	Y14	Y15	Y16	Y17	Y18	Y19	Y20	Y21	Y22	Y23	Y24	Y25
Private-Label Market																
Model Availability	100	50	52	53	0	89	.	.	.	.	.	.	.	.	.	.
Quality Rating	100	63	70	62	0	89	.	.	.	.	.	.	.	.	.	.
Bid Price	28.34	29.00	29.49	32.99	0.00	33.99	.	.	.	.	.	.	.	.	.	.
Pairs Offered	500	843	1,000	1,000	0	5,636	.	.	.	.	.	.	.	.	.	.
Pairs Sold	500	800	1,000	1,000	0	0	.	.	.	.	.	.	.	.	.	.
Market Share (%)	10.0	17.0	19.4	15.5	0.0	0.0	.	.	.	.	.	.	.	.	.	.
N.A. Branded Market																
Model Availability	100	100	142	150	135	148	.	.	.	.	.	.	.	.	.	.
Quality Rating	100	113	121	119	119	127	.	.	.	.	.	.	.	.	.	.
Service Rating	100	110	148	0	88	187	.	.	.	.	.	.	.	.	.	.
Number of Retailers	5,000	5,000	3,500	3,500	3,500	4,000	.	.	.	.	.	.	.	.	.	.
Advertising Budget	2,000	2,000	2,500	3,250	3,250	4,250	.	.	.	.	.	.	.	.	.	.
Image Rating	50	50	50	50	54	58	.	.	.	.	.	.	.	.	.	.
Customer Rebates	3	0	0	5	5	5	.	.	.	.	.	.	.	.	.	.
Selling Price	34.00	41.25	41.99	45.99	47.99	43.99	.	.	.	.	.	.	.	.	.	.
Pairs Demanded [1]	1,250	777	2,626	3,203	2,874	3,870	.	.	.	.	.	.	.	.	.	.
Pairs Sold	1,250	1,167	1,842	2,964	2,874	3,870	.	.	.	.	.	.	.	.	.	.
Market Share (%)	10.0	8.2	10.5	16.1	16.2	18.6	.	.	.	.	.	.	.	.	.	.
European Branded Market																
Model Availability	100	100	149	150	150	150	.	.	.	.	.	.	.	.	.	.
Quality Rating	100	113	124	121	115	120	.	.	.	.	.	.	.	.	.	.
Service Rating	100	115	138	44	138	203	.	.	.	.	.	.	.	.	.	.
Number of Retailers	1,000	1,100	1,000	1,000	1,000	1,000	.	.	.	.	.	.	.	.	.	.
Advertising Budget	1,000	1,000	1,000	1,500	1,500	2,500	.	.	.	.	.	.	.	.	.	.
Image Rating	50	46	46	46	50	54	.	.	.	.	.	.	.	.	.	.
Customer Rebates	2	0	0	3	3	5	.	.	.	.	.	.	.	.	.	.
Selling Price	35.00	43.50	45.99	45.99	49.99	43.99	.	.	.	.	.	.	.	.	.	.
Pairs Demanded [1]	500	317	883	1,349	1,473	2,722	.	.	.	.	.	.	.	.	.	.
Pairs Sold	500	501	694	1,339	1,489	2,722	.	.	.	.	.	.	.	.	.	.
Market Share (%)	10.0	8.6	10.4	15.4	14.6	18.9	.	.	.	.	.	.	.	.	.	.
Asian Branded Market																
Model Availability	100	100	149	149	150	150	.	.	.	.	.	.	.	.	.	.
Quality Rating	100	111	124	121	115	123	.	.	.	.	.	.	.	.	.	.
Service Rating	100	144	144	144	209	209	.	.	.	.	.	.	.	.	.	.
Number of Retailers	500	500	500	500	500	500	.	.	.	.	.	.	.	.	.	.
Advertising Budget	500	750	2,000	1,500	1,500	2,250	.	.	.	.	.	.	.	.	.	.
Image Rating	50	42	58	58	62	66	.	.	.	.	.	.	.	.	.	.
Customer Rebates	1	0	0	3	3	5	.	.	.	.	.	.	.	.	.	.
Selling Price	36.00	45.75	47.49	45.99	48.49	41.99	.	.	.	.	.	.	.	.	.	.
Pairs Demanded [1]	240	212	426	962	948	2,027	.	.	.	.	.	.	.	.	.	.
Pairs Sold	240	286	613	967	948	2,264	.	.	.	.	.	.	.	.	.	.
Market Share (%)	10.0	8.6	13.6	17.6	10.6	15.9	.	.	.	.	.	.	.	.	.	.

[1] Pairs Demanded = Pairs Sold + Stockouts – Sales Gained from Stockouts. This is the truest measure of the demand generated by a company's competitive strategy, since stockouts represent unsatisfied demand and sales gains from stockouts are a windfall resulting from the demand misjudgements of rivals.

Note: Companies with sales of fewer than 100,000 pairs are not included in industry averages, except for pairs demanded, pairs sold, and market share.

Appendix B

PLANNING AND ANALYSIS FORMS

Provided in this section are several blank forms intended to help you organize and plan your company's strategy and operations, and analyze the industry in which you are competing.

COMPANY MISSION AND OBJECTIVES

The Business Strategy Game

Industry ___ **Company** ___

1. MISSION STATEMENT / STRATEGIC VISION

____
____
____
____
____
____
____
____

2. MARKET SHARE OBJECTIVES

Private-Label Market		____ %
Branded Markets ——	North America	____ %
	Europe	____ %
	Asia	____ %
Worldwide (overall market share objective)		____ %

3. LONG-TERM FINANCIAL PERFORMANCE OBJECTIVES

Growth in Revenues	____ %
Growth in Net Income	____ %
Growth in Earnings Per Share	____ %
Return on Stockholders' Equity	____ %
Bond Rating	____

4. ANNUAL FINANCIAL PERFORMANCE OBJECTIVES

	Year ___	Year ___	Year ___	Year ___	Year ___
Revenues	$ ____	$ ____	$ ____	$ ____	$ ____
Net Income	$ ____	$ ____	$ ____	$ ____	$ ____
Earnings Per Share	$ ____	$ ____	$ ____	$ ____	$ ____
Return On Equity	____ %	____ %	____ %	____ %	____ %
Bond Rating	____	____	____	____	____

COMPANY STRATEGY

The Business Strategy Game

Industry ___ **Company ___**

1. PRIMARY MARKET TARGETS (rank 1 to 4 in order of importance)

Private-Label Market		☐
Branded Markets ——	North America	☐
	Europe	☐
	Asia	☐

2. OVERALL COMPETITIVE POSITIONING (check appropriate boxes and fill in blanks)

Price Relative to Competitors

- Premium ☐
- Above Average ☐
- Average ☐
- Below Average ☐
- Lowest ☐

Product Quality

- Top of the Line ☐
- Premium ☐
- Good ☐
- Acceptable ☐
- Rank in Industry ___

Service to Retailers

- Superior ☐
- Above Average ☐
- Standard ☐
- Rank in Industry ___

Brand Image (image rating)

- High Profile ☐
- Moderate ☐
- Low Profile ☐
- Rank In Industry ___

Product Line Breadth (models)

- Broad ☐
- Medium ☐
- Narrow ☐
- Rank in Industry ___

Number of Retail Outlets

- Above Average ☐
- Average ☐
- Below Average ☐
- Rank In Industry ___

Advertising Budget

- Above Average ☐
- Average ☐
- Below Average ☐
- Rank in Industry ___

Use of Customer Rebates

- Heavy ☐
- Medium ☐
- Light ☐
- Rank In Industry ___

COMPANY STRATEGY
(continued)

3. OVERALL BUSINESS STRATEGY (check appropriate box and explain)

		Competitive Advantage Being Sought
Low-Cost	☐	
Differentiation	☐	
Focus	☐	
Best-Cost	☐	

4. ACTIONS TO GAIN COMPETITIVE ADVANTAGE (explain)

5. SPECIAL FUNCTIONAL AREA STRATEGIES (explain)

Production

Marketing

Finance

Human Resources

INDUSTRY AND COMPETITIVE ANALYSIS

The Business Strategy Game

Industry ___ **Company ___**

1. DOMINANT ECONOMIC CHARACTERISTICS (explain)

____

____

____

____

____

2. DRIVING FORCES (explain)

____

____

____

____

____

3. ASSESSMENT OF COMPETITIVE FORCES (explain)

____

____

____

____

____

4. STRENGTH OF KEY COMPETITORS (Rating Scale: 1 = weakest; 10 = strongest)

Competitive Factor	**Our Company**	**Key Competitors** (company name or letter)						
		____	____	____	____	____	____	____
Low-Cost	____	____	____	____	____	____	____	____
Model Availability	____	____	____	____	____	____	____	____
Quality	____	____	____	____	____	____	____	____
Service	____	____	____	____	____	____	____	____
Retail Outlets	____	____	____	____	____	____	____	____
Brand Image	____	____	____	____	____	____	____	____
Management Expertise	____	____	____	____	____	____	____	____
Overall Strength Rating	____	____	____	____	____	____	____	____

Industry and Competitive Analysis

(continued)

5. Strategic Group Map — North America

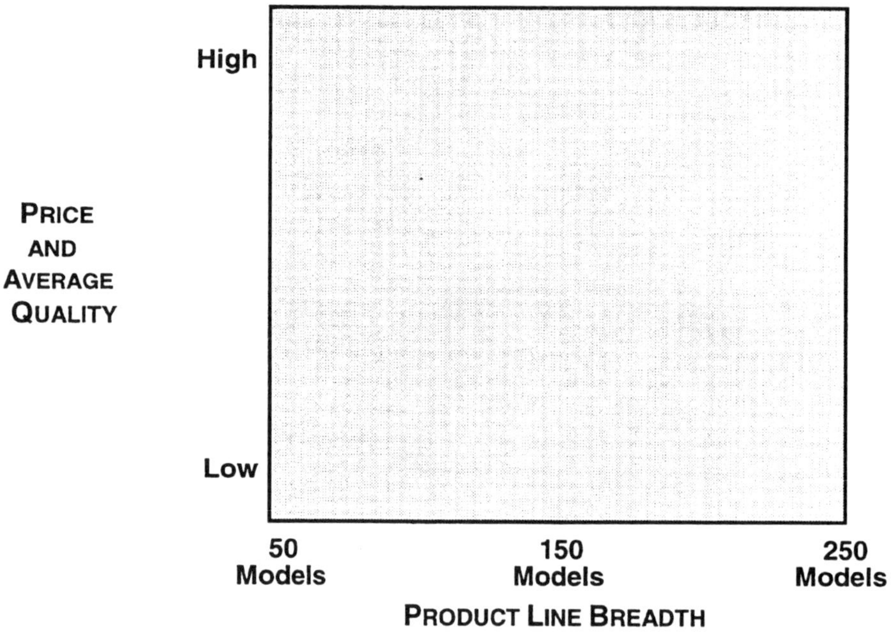

6. Strategic Group Map — Europe

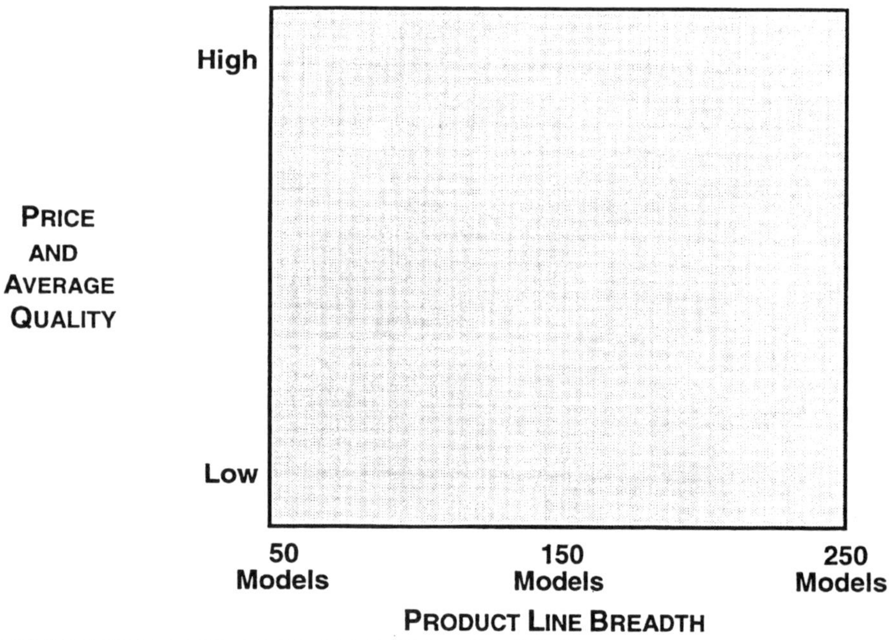

Industry and Competitive Analysis
(continued)

7. Strategic Group Map — Asia

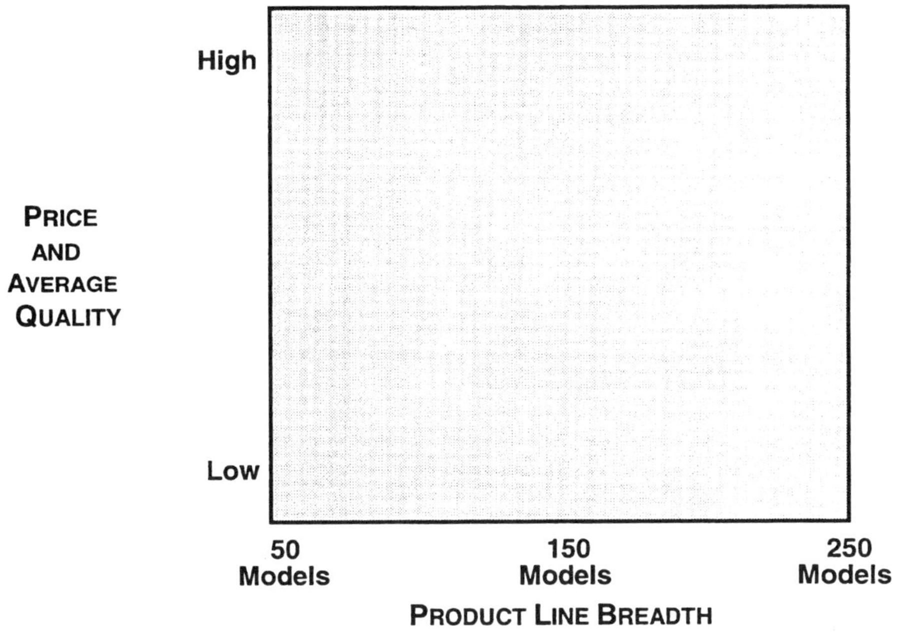

8. Key Success Factors (explain)

____

____

____

____

____

____

____

9. Industry Prospects and Overall Attractiveness (explain)

____

____

____

____

____

____

____

Index

A

Accounts Payable — 36, 37
Accounts Receivable — 36, 37
Accumulated Depreciation
  Reported in Balance Sheet — 37
  Reported (by plant) in Manufacturing Report — 18, 23
Accumulated Retained Earnings
  Impact of stock retirement — 68
  Reported in Balance Sheet — 37
Additional Stockholders' Capital
  Impact of stock issue/retirement — 66, 68
  Reported in Balance Sheet — 37
Administrative Expenses — 30, 31
Advertising
  Decision entries — 59, 60
  Cumulative impact on image rating — 15
  Expense reported in Marketing and Administrative Report — 30
  Market share impact — 15
Annual Wage — see Compensation
Automation Options
  Decision entries — 53, 54
  Reported in Manufacturing Report — 18, 24

B

Balance Sheet — 36 through 38
Beginning Cash Balance — see Cash Balance
Beginning Inventory — see Inventory
Benchmarking Report
  Explanation — 79
  Sample report — 101
Bids for New Celebrity Endorsement Contracts — 64, 65
Bonds
  Decision entries — 66, 67
  Interest rates — 66
  Outstanding issues reported in Balance Sheet — 37

Bond Rating
Impact on access to additional debt — 67
Impact on company interest rates — 66
Projected on Financial Decisions Screen — 67
Scoring variable explanation — 76
Variables impacting bond rating — 36
Brand Image — 15, 65,
Branded Marketing Decisions
Decision entries — 59, 60, 61
Market share impact — 11 through 16

C

Capacity — see PLANT CAPACITY
Capacity Utilization
Impact on materials prices — 10
Maximum plant capacity utilization — 12, 24
Cash Balance
Beginning and ending balance reported in Cash Flow Report — 38, 39
Interest income earned — 39, 68
Shortfall arrangements and penalties — 68
Cash Flow Report — 38, 39
Cash Inflows — see CASH FLOW REPORT
Cash On Hand — see CASH BALANCE
Cash Outflows — see CASH FLOW REPORT
Celebrity Endorsements
Bids for new celebrity endorsement contracts — 64, 65
Impact on Image Rating — 15
Common Stock — see STOCK
Company Letter — 83
Company Name — 83
Compensation
Annual base wages
Impact on productivity — 20, 21
Minimum wages — 21, 50
Reported in Manufacturing Report — 18
Wage increases — 20, 50
Decision entries — 49, 50
Incentive pay
Impact on productivity — 20, 21, 50
Impact on reject rates — 22, 48
Reported in Manufacturing Report — 18
Total compensation package
Impact on productivity — 20
Reported in Manufacturing Report — 18
Company Reports
Containing current-year results
Accessing and printing — 80
Explained — 17 through 39
Projected for upcoming year — 85
Competitor Analysis Reports
Explanation — 79, 80
Sample report — 102, 103
Corporate Overhead — 31
Cost Report — 32 through 35
Costs and Rates — 43, 44
Cost of Faster Delivery — see DELIVERY COST
Cumulative Advertising Expenditures
Impact on Image Rating — 15
Cumulative Quality Control Expenditures — see QUALITY CONTROL
Customer Rebates
Decision entries — 59, 60
Expenses reported in Marketing and Administrative Report — 30
Market share impact — 16
Customer Service Reps
Decision entries — 59, 60
Expenses reported in Marketing and Administrative Report — 30
Impact on service rating — 13, 60

D

Debt-To-Assets Ratio
Defined and explained — 36
Decision Entries
Accessing — 44, 85
Explained — 44 through 73
Printing — 72
Recommended decision-making procedure — 86, 87, 88
Delivery Costs — 30, 31, 60
Delivery Time
Decision entries — 59, 60
Impact on service rating — 14
Demand
Expected growth for Years 11 through 15 — 7
Forecasting — see DEMAND FORECASTING MODEL

Projections for Years 11 and 12 — 7, 8, 45
Reported in Warehouse and Sales Report — 24, 25
Variables impacting a company's market share — 11 through 16, 61, 62
Variables impacting industry-wide demand — 8, 9

Demand Forecasting Model — 61, 62, 63

Depreciation
Reported in Manufacturing Report — 18, 25
See ACCUMULATED DEPRECIATION

Dividends
Accounting Impact — 69
Decision entries — 67, 69
Impact on stock price — 69, 70
Payments reported in Cash Flow Report — 39, 39

E

Earnings Per Share
Impact on stock price — 69, 70
Scoring variable explanation — 76, 77, 78

Ending Inventory — see INVENTORY

EPS — see EARNINGS PER SHARE

Eurodollar — see EXCHANGE RATES

Exchange Rates
Adjustments report in Warehouse and Sales Report — 25 through 28
Changes in Japanese Yen and Eurodollar — 43, 44

Executive Compensation
Optional Decision Entries Screen — 70 through 72
Reported on the Marketing and Administrative Report — 30, 31

Expansion of Plants — see PLANT EXPANSION

Extra Bond Payment — see BONDS

Extraordinary Gain (Loss) from Capacity Sale/Closing
Reported in Income Statement — 35
See PLANT CAPACITY SALE
See PERMANENT CAPACITY SHUTDOWN

F

Financial Decisions — 65 through 70

FIR — see FOOTWEAR INDUSTRY REPORT

Five-Year Strategic Plan
Accessing and printing — 85
Explained — 80

Footwear Industry Report
Explanation and printing — 78, 79
Sample report — 90 through 100

Freight Charges on Footwear Shipments — 25, 29

G

Geographic Profit Report — 31, 32

I

Image Rating
Explanation — 15, 65
Market share impact — 15

Import Tariffs — see TARIFFS

Income After Taxes
Reported in Income Statement — 35
Scoring variable explanation — 75 through 78

Income Taxes
Reported in Cash Flow Report — 38, 39
Reported in Income Statement — 35
Tax rate — 36

Industry Number — 83, 84

Interest
Expense reported in Income Statement — 35
Income earned on cash balances — 68
Payments reported in Cash Flow Report — 38, 39

Interest Rates
Long-term (bonds) — 66
Short-term — 66, 68

Inventory
Beginning footwear inventory
Impact on quality rating — 13
Reported in Warehouse and Sales Report — 25
Ending footwear inventory
Impact on delivery time — 60, 61
Impact on service rating — 14

Reported in Warehouse and Sales Report — 25
Storage charges — 25, 28, 29, 52, 61
Inventory cost adjustment — 33, 34
Liquidation — see INVENTORY LIQUIDATION OPTION
Storage Costs — 28, 29, 52, 61

Inventory Liquidation Option
Decision entries — 63, 64
Reported in Geographic Profit Report — 33

J

Japanese Yen — see EXCHANGE RATES

L

Labor
Costs reported in Manufacturing Report — 18, 19
Decision entries — 49 through 51
See COMPENSATION

Labor Productivity — see PRODUCTIVITY
Liquidation Value — 54
Long-Term Debt — see BONDS
Long-Wear Materials — see MATERIALS

M

Main Menu — 84, 85
Maintenance Costs — see PLANT MAINTENANCE
Manufacturing Cost of Goods Sold
Reported in Income Statement — 35
Reported in Warehouse and Sales Report — 25, 26

Manufacturing Cost Per Pair Produced — 32, 33
Manufacturing Costs — 18 through 23
Manufacturing Decisions — 44 through 49
Manufacturing Report — 18 through 24
Marketing and Administrative Report — 30, 31
Marketing Decisions — see BRANDED MARKETING DECISIONS or PRIVATE-LABEL MARKETING DECISIONS
Materials
Decision entries — 45, 46
Expenses reported in Manufacturing Report — 18, 19
Impact on quality rating — 12, 13
Prices
Making what-if estimates — 48
Variables impacting materials prices — 10, 11

Model Availability
Explained — 16, 46
Market share impact — 16,
Minimum requirement for private-label participation — 13, 57, 58

Models
Decision entries — 45, 46, 47
Impact on production run set-up costs — 23, 46
Impact on quality rating — 12, 13
Impact on reject rates — 22, 48

N

New Plants — see PLANT CONSTRUCTION
Net Income — see INCOME AFTER TAXES
Normal-Wear Materials — see MATERIALS
Number of Models — see MODELS

O

On-Time Delivery — see DELIVERY
Order Filling Costs — see WAREHOUSE OVERHEAD
Overhead — see CORPORATE OVERHEAD or WAREHOUSE OVERHEAD
Overtime
Decision entries — 45, 46, 49
Expenses reported in Manufacturing Report — 18, 19, 21

P

Password — 83
Permanent Capacity Shutdown
Decision entries — 54, 55
Extraordinary loss (write-off) reported in Income Statement — 35, 36
Liquidation cash inflow reported in Cash Flow Report — 38

Piecework Incentive — see COMPENSATION

Plant Capacity
Reported in Manufacturing Report — 18, 23, 24
See CAPACITY UTILIZATION
Plant Capacity Shutdown
Permanent — 36, 38, 54, 55
Temporary — 57
Plant Construction (new)
Cost — 55
Decision entries — 54, 55, 56
Reported in Manufacturing Report — 18, 23, 24
Plant Decisions — 53 through 57
Plant Expansion
Cost — 55
Decision entries — 54, 55, 56
Reported in Manufacturing Report — 18, 23, 24
Plant Investment
Cost of new plant construction and capacity expansion — 55
Reported in Balance Sheet — 36, 37
Reported in Manufacturing Report — 18, 23,
Plant Life — 23, 55
Plant Maintenance — 18, 23
Plant Size
Expansion limitations — 56
New construction limitations — 55
Price — see WHOLESALE PRICE TO RETAILERS
Private-Label
Bidding parameters and requirements — 9, 57, 58
Conversion of unsold pairs to North American branded — 57, 58
Demand Forecast for Years 11 and 12 — 8, 45
Market share allocation explained — 9, 57
Private-Label Marketing Decisions — 57, 58, 59
Production Methods Improvements
Decision entries — 45, 47, 48
Impact on materials costs — 23, 47, 48
Impact on plant supervision costs — 23, 47, 48
Impact on productivity — 23, 47, 48
Reported in Manufacturing Report — 18, 23
Production Quality — see QUALITY RATING
Production Run Set-Up Cost — 18, 23
Productivity
Impact of production methods improvements expenditures — 23, 47, 48
Impact of worker compensation — 20, 50
Making what-if projections — 50, 51
Reported in Manufacturing Report — 18, 20
Product Line Breadth
Market share impact — 16
See MODEL AVAILABILITY

Q

Quality Control
Decision entries — 45, 47
Expenses reported in Manufacturing Report — 18, 22
Impact on reject rates — 22, 47
Impact on quality rating — 13, 47
Quality Rating
Market share impact — 12, 13
Minimum requirement for Private-Label participation — see PRIVATE-LABEL
Quality of inventory carried over — 13, 59
Reported in Manufacturing Report — 18
Variables impacting quality rating — 12, 13

R

Raw Materials — see MATERIALS
Rebates — see CUSTOMER REBATES
Reject Rates
Making what-if projections — 45, 48
Reported in Manufacturing Report — 18
Variables impacting reject rates — 22
Retail Outlets
Decision entries — 59, 60
Expenses reported in Marketing and Administrative Report — 30
Impact on service rating — 14,
Market share impact — 14
Return On Equity
Impact on stock price — 69
Scoring variable explanation — 75 through 78
Revenues — see SALES REVENUES

S

S&P 500 Index — 8, 44
Sales Forecast — see DEMAND or WHAT-IF ESTIMATES
Sales Revenues
Impact on stock price — 69
Reported in Income Statement — 38, 39
Scoring variable explanation — 75 through 78
Selling Price — see WHOLESALE PRICE TO RETAILERS
Service Rating
Market share impact — 14, 15
Variables impacting service rating — 14, 15
Shipping Costs — see FREIGHT CHARGES
Shipping Decisions — 51, 52, 53
Short-Term Loan
Computer generated loans — 66
Decision entry — 66, 67
Interest rate — 65, 66
Reported in Balance Sheet — 36, 37
Reported in Cash Flow Report — 38, 39
Stock
Issues — 66
Retirement — 67, 68
Shares Outstanding
Maximum — 37
Minimum — 37, 68
Reported in Balance Sheet — 37
Stockouts
Defined/explained — 24
Impact on service rating — 14, 15
Reported in Warehouse and Sales Report — 25
Stock Price
Variables impacting stock price — 69
Stock Value
Scoring variable explained — 75 through 78
Storage Charges — 25, 28, 29, 52, 61
Strategic Plan — see FIVE-YEAR STRATEGIC PLAN
Strategy Rating — 75 through 78
Styling/Features Budget
Decision entries — 45, 47
Expense reported in Manufacturing Report — 18, 22, 23
Impact on quality rating — 12, 13

T

Tariffs — 25, 29
Temporary Plant Shutdowns — 57
Times-Interest-Earned Ratio
Impact on bond rating — 36, 37, 38,
Minimum requirement for new bond issues — 37, 67

W

Wages — see COMPENSATION
Warehouse and Sales Report — 24 through 30
Warehouse Expenses — 25, 28, 29, 30
Warehouse Operating Costs — 25, 29, 30
What-If Estimates
Branded sales estimates — 59, 61, see DEMAND FORECASTING MODEL
Materials cost estimates — 45, 48
Private-label sales estimate — 58, 59
Reject rate estimates — 45, 48
Worker productivity — 50, 51
Wholesale Price to Retailers
Decision entries — 59, 60
Market share impact — 12
Worker Pay — see COMPENSATION
Worker Productivity — see PRODUCTIVITY